# Stephen Neale

# CAMPING BY THE WATERSIDE

## The best campsites by water in Britain and Ireland

ADLARD COLES NAUTICAL

BLOOMSBURY

LONDON · NEW DELHI · NEW YORK · SYDNEY

For Mum and Dad & Deb and Romi

Published by Adlard Coles Nautical
an imprint of Bloomsbury Publishing Plc
50 Bedford Square, London WC1B 3DP
www.adlardcoles.com

First published by Adlard Coles Nautical in 2013

ISBN 978-1-4081-6069-5
ePDF 978-1-4081-6179-1
ePub 978-1-4081-6178-4

A CIP catalogue record for this book is available from the British Library.

This book is produced using paper that is made from wood grown in managed, sustainable forests.
It is natural, renewable and recyclable. The logging and manufacturing processes conform to the
environmental regulations of the country of origin.

Typeset in 9 pt Glyphs by James Watson
Printed and bound in China by RRD South China

**Note**: While the author and publisher of this book have gone to great lengths to ensure the accuracy
of the information contained herein, they will not be held legally or financially responsible for any
accident, injury, loss or inconvenience sustained, or for actions taken (or not taken), as a result of this
information. Taking part in any of the activities described in this book is entirely at your own risk.

## Acknowledgements
Photos in Part 1 show the following sites (left to right, top to bottom):
p9 Uig; Rushbanks; Grindley Brook. p12 Sands; Lakeside Touring Park. p14 Uig; Cornwall. p16 wild
camping in Bath; Arisaig. p19 Sands; Wexford Harbour. p20 Harris; wild camping near Barmouth.
p23 Wexford. p25 Cornwall. p27 Tramore, Ireland. p29 New Forest; Skegness; Sumner Ponds;
Westerley Lake. p33 Sands; Uig. p35 Uig; Lincolnshire. p37 Uig; Lucksall. p45 Wexford.

All photos © Stephen Neale / Romi Neale except:
p14 (bottom – lady with frisbee) © Barney Moss; p20 (right) © Mark Floutier / John Floutier Sailing
Canoes; p25 (top) and p137 (top right), © Geraint Morgan; p25 (bottom) © Ian Griffiths; p49 (top)
© Corey Taratuta/www.IrishFireside.com; p51 (top) © Michael Clarke; p52 © Mark Heard; p53 ©
Hidden Valley Park; p59 (top) © Mortimer Moriarty; p59 (bottom) © Stephen Malone; p67, p197
(bottom) © Caravan Club; p78 © Kevin Millican; p79 © Graham Robertson; p80 © Camping and
Caravanning Club; p83 (bottom left – man jumping in dunes) © Richard Child; p103 (top) © Gareth
Lovering; p137 (top left) © Tony Bond; p141 (top right) © Geoff Pugh/Giant Pixel Photography; p142
© Suzanne Hall; p163 © Jon Pennycook; p191 © Thomas Marshall.

Photos on pages 3, 8, 18, 44, 48 (bottom right), 51 (bottom left and right), 58, 108, 109 (top right and
bottom right) 157 (bottom) 196, 197 (top) 232 and 233 (top right and bottom left) © Shutterstock

## Special thanks
To Martin Dalton and Mark Cleveland for photographic guidance, especially Martin for his editing
and filing advice; all the excellent photographers who so kindly offered pictures that sadly did not
make it into these pages; Martin Dorey for so generously writing the Foreword and motivating me
to get writing; John Kelly for his superb Song of the Paddle forum, and lastly, Terry Abraham, the
blogger and film maker, who constantly shares his knowledge and passion for the outdoors with the
rest of us.

# contents

## part 1 *laying the groundwork*

## part 2 *regional guides*

# foreword

Stephen's premise for finding a good campsite is spot on. What more could you ask than to cast your line or launch your kayak from right outside your tent or camper van? For me, as a surfer, campervanner and coast lover, finding places where you can pitch up at the edge of the water really is the Holy Grail. It's what we dream of. To be able to roll out of bed and into the surf is what it's all about. That's proper camping. The best start to any day. Then, once the waves or the fish or the rays have been caught, you can pop the kettle on, cook up your catch or just take it easy, right there at the very edge, where the sea meets the land, where it matters.

It's not that easy to come across campsites that are right on the water, with the right kind of facilities and the right kind of vibe. So it's absolutely brilliant that Stephen is willing and able to share the fruits of his long quest to find the very best of them in this book. I've been to a few of them myself and can understand why he'd want to write them all down. These are the places that make you go 'wow!'

Stephen has taken the hard work out of locating your own pitch in paradise. And when I say paradise I don't mean just a hop, skip and a jump away, or even just a stone's throw from paradise, I mean right there. That's what it's all about.

I only wish I'd thought of it first.
Martin Dorey

Martin Dorey is a Devon based writer. His book *The Camper Van Cookbook*, which was released in 2010, has been hailed as 'a modern outdoor classic'. It inspired the BBC2 TV series *One Man and his Campervan*, which saw Martin travelling the length and breadth of Britain cooking, foraging and having fun in his beloved 1970s VW camper van. Stephen contributed his list of the ten best campsites on water for Martin's second book, *The Camper Van Coast*, published in 2012.

# preface

I had a chat with a canoeist one day.

'Imagine this,' he said, as he packed up his gear. 'Sliding your canoe onto the river from right next to your own tent. Jumping into the sea from the bonnet of your camper. Or how about casting a fishing line into the lake from inside your caravan awning?'

So I started looking.

# part 1
## laying the groundwork

# getting ready

**I'll tell you a secret. These islands are the best in the world to go camping. It's not a 'Da Vinci Code', Dan Brown-style revelation. But it does involve multiples of the number three. Britain and Ireland are an archipelago of 6,000 islands divided and surrounded by six seas, 600 rivers and canals and 30,000 lakes. They are home to more campsites-by-water per square mile than anywhere else on earth. Only no one realised, or if they did, they've kept it quiet.**

Why? I've no idea, because these regions also enjoy the mildest seasons found anywhere (neither hot nor cold – posh people call it temperate). So mild, in fact, that the three largest camping organisations in the world are based here, with a total membership of almost six million. Those who should know better still stop me and ask what's so special about a pitch by the water. They might describe a wonderful campsite in the Yorkshire Dales, the New Forest or Snowdonia, several miles from a river or lake, but stunningly beautiful. 'Well, yeah,' I whisper. 'Maybe when the sun's out. What about when it rains every day for a week?'

Demystifying the myths about camping and caravanning in a damp corner of the northern hemisphere is a challenge. It's not all good, I'll grant you. Pitched up at the foot of the Dales in a three-day downpour surrounded by grazing Fresians, puddles and damp ditches can be depressing. But the combination of lake, wetsuit, boats, fishing rods and campsite amounts to fun in any weather. Canoeing, sailing, surfing, swimming and snorkelling don't rely on sunshine – they rely on access to a beach or riverbank. And that's what the campsites in this book have. They get you out there.

Until now, most have been kept secret and treasured by the people 'in the know'. And for good reason. No one wants to discover a waterside gem only to see it become over-run with hundreds of tents, campervans, windbreaks, people and 24-hour noise.  So I spent five years looking. Looking for those secret hideaways. I did it by trawling around coasts, rivers and lakes.

It all started from the armchair. Staring at OS Maps and staying up into the early hours on Google Earth, using a computer screen to fly over canals and lakes, searching for anything that resembled a tent or caravan. Once a dozen sites had been saved in my favourites, I'd head off for a long weekend of camping, sometimes driving all night to explore the area by day. Within four years I'd discovered more than one thousand campsites – way too many to worry about keeping them secret any longer. From the Gold Coast of County Waterford to the dunes of North Devon, from the Norfolk Broads to the turquoise waters of the Outer Hebrides and the Pembrokeshire path – Britain and Ireland are teeming with great spots to camp by water. And the best news of all is that the list just keeps growing and getting better. Every time I get the map out, more campsites have appeared.

And then there's the water. Quality has improved dramatically in the last decade. Rivers and canals once polluted by the legacy of the industrial revolution have become the cleanest waterways in Europe. Save for issues caused by extreme flooding and rainfall in 2012, many beaches are returning to safe levels, largely thanks to superb campaigns by the likes of Surfers Against Sewage. For the first time in more than 150 years, it's relatively safe to go wild swimming in Britain.

Modern camping is not just about getting back to nature either – there's a whole lot of new 'stuff' to embrace, too. Aside from Wi-Fi and sat-nav-enabled phones, improvements in fabric technology are the most important developments for the 21st-century camper. This is the dawn of an outdoor revolution. Gortex, eVent and battery-heated wetsuits make it easy to take on the coldest waters all-year round – even in sub-zero temperatures. For every cloud hanging over these isles, there's the silver lining of waterways, lakes, coast, canvas and caravans. Oh, and we get some sunshine too.

The British Isles (including Ireland) are surrounded by six seas – the south and north English Channels, the North Sea, the Atlantic Ocean, the Irish Sea and the Celtic Sea.

## Get the gear

The gear I mention here is not always the cheapest, but I consider it the best value for money. In most cases you will only need to buy it once, whereas cheap gear will turn out to be a false economy. Much of this stuff can be found on eBay, sometimes for half price or less. Old-stock eVent and Gortex does the same job in 2013 as it was designed to do in 2009. I've seen some of the gear listed above (not wetsuits) being sold off second-hand in charity shops and pawn outlets. The former is always a bargain; the latter requires an ability to haggle hard with the owner (not a sales assistant) while holding a wad of crisp cash. Failing that, sell off the golf clubs or the second car, start making sandwiches to take to work and invest the cash in a new way of life, next to nature.

## Wetsuits

Keeping warm in the water can be a challenge, even in the summer months, and winter is another problem altogether. Having the right clothing, shelter and bedding is crucial to discovering the British and Irish backwaters all year round. Let's start right in the water. Wetsuits and surface drysuits are a relatively cheap solution to staying dry and warm, even in the middle of January. Whatever you spend, make sure you find a perfect fit before you buy. Don't buy online, unless you have tried the suit on somewhere first, as sizes vary from manufacturer to manufacturer.

For swimming in seas and rivers, triathlon suits are generally best. They can be bought for less than £100 or hired very cheaply for a whole summer season. For surface sports, thick wetsuits are ideal. Rip Curl have the Flash Bomb, which will dry out in two hours. For surfing during the coldest of winters, you will need a wetsuit of the thickest synthetic rubber, known as neoprene. If you want a wetsuit for all seasons, go for neoprene that is 5 mm or 4 mm thick. For just winter use, 6 mm is best. One of the warmest suits is the Xcel Infinite Drylock with a hood, but the Gul Vortex

Steamer is a cheaper alternative. I wear 7 mm Gul booties and five-mm Gul gloves. An even cheaper, but excellent-value suit is the Billabong Foil 5/3 mm Chest Zip Wetsuit. The Rip Curl H-Bomb is a battery-powered, heated wetsuit, designed for wimps like me who really feel the cold. It's not cheap, but it keeps surfers or kayakers toasty for three hours in icy cold water. The value alternatives are the Rip Curl H-Bomb heated vest (powered by battery, but safe in water), which can be worn underneath a much cheaper all-year wetsuit, or the QuikSilver Cypher heated vest.

Most winter sailors and kayakers use surface drysuits. For a few hundred pounds, they keep people dry in the event of a capsize, but are easier to move about in than a wetsuit. Top of the range is the Musto HPX Ocean Dry Suit. It's expensive, but it's designed to keep people alive for several hours in freezing weather. If it can do that, it sounds like a bargain.

## Clothing

Traditional outdoor clothing is OK in and around water when there's no chance of taking an unexpected dip. Unlike wetsuits, the fabric's main function is to keep rainwater out, while letting warm air escape. Some jackets are semi-breathable and 100% waterproof. They're commonly known as 'hard shells'. Gortex is the most popular, thanks to some good marketing, but there are lesser-known and sometimes cheaper products that can do the job. Look for fabrics such as eVent, HyVent, Nikwax and Entrant DT – there are many more, too. For all the claims made about the breathable properties of hard shells, the reality is that unless clothing is well-vented by the wearer, condensation can often form on the inside, making them wet. It can be very frustrating to spend over £200 on a jacket, to feel moisture creeping its way up your arm. So either vent or look for alternatives (avoiding hard shells). I go for the latter.

My winter system involves wearing a minimum of three breathable layers, with a base layer that removes moisture from the skin (known as wicking). The best base layers are Merino or Helly Hanson woollens –  they work hard to keep you dry and warm. Over the base layer, I wear a polyester fleece. These can be bought for about £10, or even less if you find one in a charity shop. I typically wear a 200g fleece in winter. Over that goes a soft pertex shell, which is extremely breathable, with a Primaloft quilt for warmth. The jacket I wear is the Berghaus Ignite Hooded Jacket, which costs less than £100. It easily copes at temperatures well-below freezing, and because it's breathable I rarely sweat unless I've put on a fleece that is too thick. It's also semi-waterproof, which means it can cope with heavy showers but won't keep out all-day torrential rainfall. And that's why I carry a lightweight hard shell for those very few occasions each year when it rains all day. It can be thrown over the top of the Helly Hanson and fleece or the Berghaus Ignite on a really cold day. The most important thing is to keep it vented by opening the front zip as much as possible. The jacket I use is the Montane Venture. It's made of eVent, which in my opinion is one of the best fabrics on the market. A cheaper alternative is the Montane Atomic. For hard shell trousers, I wear Montane Atomic DT Pants. Shoes and boots are relative to the job in hand, although Muckboots are excellent all-purpose kit for camping.

## Shelter

When it comes to shelter, I err on the side of extravagance by using a motorhome. But in fine weather, less is more. The ultimate outdoor experience is a hammock, underneath tarp (see Ray Mears). Bivvying – camping inside a tiny tent like shelter (the size of a giant sleeping bag) designed to just protect a single person from the elements – is the next best thing for purists. There are some fantastic bivouac shelters on the market, some for less than £200. I've got a Rab Ridge Raider bivvy made of eVent. It's a fully waterproof and breathable wrap that allows me to slide inside with my sleeping bag and gaze skyward. Anglers are using this option more than ever for overnight expeditions

Tents remain the commonest form of camping for most people. A cheap circular pop-up tent is great in the summer for a one-night expedition.

For rainy nights, when the winds can get up a bit, there are a huge number of outstanding tents to choose from. There are plenty of bad ones, too, so do your research and experiment by borrowing from friends. The Hilleberg range really takes some beating. I tried out a Hilleberg Nammatj 2 last year – it is easy to pitch and withstands more than most. When it starts to blow above 50 miles per hour consider either looking for natural shelter or, as a last resort, ask for shelter from someone like me – in a motorhome.

## Sleeping

Sleeping bags are the other essential gear for protecting campers from the elements. Being cold inside an expensive tent is just silly, so don't cut corners on bags. There's nothing worse than shivering at night, miles from home. Go for the warmest quilt you can afford and make sure it has a pertex-type shell. This will deflect any water (condensation) that might fall in from the roof of your tent, tarp or bivouac.

# About the campsites

Apart from being home to thousands of islands, Britain and Ireland have some of the most rugged, indented coastlines in the world. We may be a small collective of isles, but if our combined coastline was stretched into a straight line it would reach more than 23,000 miles, almost the entire circumference of the earth. Add to that 30,000 lochs and lakes, and 7,000 miles of rivers and canals. Nowhere in Britain and Ireland is more than a 20-minute drive from water.

There are essentially three types of camping ground to choose from: those managed by clubs, those privately owned by commercial companies and individuals, and wild camping.

## Members' clubs

Members' club sites tend to be more consistent in their provision and are usually better regulated. Because there are more of them, they offer great access to waterways and beaches.

The Camping and Caravanning Club is the oldest camping organisation in the world, with more than 500,000 members. The Caravan Club is the largest camping club, with almost one million members. Both clubs run about 300 main sites and 4,000 smaller sites known as Certificated Locations (CLs) or Certificated Sites (CSs). The main sites can be expensive in the high season. The smaller sites have fewer facilities (usually just electricity, water and wastewater disposal), but quite a few have toilets and even showers. These certificated sites are only legally allowed to hold five pitches. For me, they are what camping is all about. Back to nature, back to basics and a chance to explore a tiny envelope of Britain in beautiful peace. We stayed on a Caravan Club CL within a few hours of buying our first motorhome, and will never forget it. Back then we paid £2.50 (no electricity or showers) but it was a wonderful adventure. Many campers choose these smaller sites over full-services sites because they offer both peaceful seclusion and great value for money. They are the best reason for joining one of these two clubs.

Some people belong to both members' clubs, although unless you camp at least 10 times a year (including weekends), I don't think it's cost-effective. Annual membership is about £40 per year, plus the cost of a night's camping. The certificated sites usually start from about £6. The largest sites will cost about £35 per night for a family in peak season, which may not seem cheap, but is excellent value considering the quality of the locations. Both operate campsites that are open all year. They are attempting to encourage more people to camp in winter, when sites are cheaper and less crowded.

We are home to the three largest and oldest camping organisations in the world, with six million members.

Britain has more coast, per ratio of landmass, than countries such as Antarctica, China, Canada, Indonesia, Australia, Russia, and America.

Another membership option is The National Trust. It's bigger than both of the two clubs mentioned above, with 3.8 million members, but it isn't really considered a 'camping' organisation. Even so, it owns about 50 campsites, and many more are on the way. The charity is one of the largest landowners in the UK, managing 630,000 acres of countryside, including a quarter of the Lake District and one-fifth of the coast in England, Wales and Northern Ireland (700 miles). The National Trust has revealed a plan to create a network of new 'simple campsites' in what it described as 'stunning locations', describing it as a 'major shift' to promote camping, walking, kayaking, surfing and cycling. In 2011 it also launched Project Neptune, a plan to buy more land.

## Commercial campsites

Commercial campsites range from a dozen pitches in a farmer's field to the largest holiday parks, run by the likes of Havens, Park Resorts, Hoseasons and John Fowler. In my experience, commercials collectively represent the best and worst of what's out there.

### A note on prices

The camping scene, like everything in life, is in a constant state of change. Prices aren't included in these campsite reviews because they fluctuate so much from year to year. The best-value campsite one year is just as likely to push pitch fees up above its competitors the next year, and vice versa. Many owners of certificated sites aspire to become small campsites. Small campsites are applying for seasonal pitches. Seasonals are applying for three or four statics. And static caravan parks are turning away tourers and applying for residential status. The entire process from CL to residential park can take several decades, but it's no less upsetting seeing your favourite site disappear. You may not like it, but for every campsite and touring park this year that decides to stop hosting tents or tourers, there will be another hundred farmers, landowners, entrepreneurs or dreamers who will apply for camping status in some equally stunning spots.

## Wild camping

Club and commercial sites provide tens of thousands of pitches within a few steps of shoreline, riverbank or beach. But if there's no campsite in the specific area you want to visit, there's one last option. Wild camping is legal in Scotland, but in England, Wales and Ireland, apart from a few exceptions, permission is needed from the landowner. Wild camping represents everything that is good and bad about living outside socially accepted conventions. Knowing both your rights and responsibilities is important. Conflict with landowners, locals, enforcement officials and police is common. The most experienced wild campers have learnt to remain polite, courteous and calm, choosing to move on rather than agitate situations where a reasonable compromise cannot be reached. At its best, wild camping is a fun way for the responsible camper to enjoy the most remote scenery in peace.

The definition of true wild camping refers to the practice of isolated camping alone in a tent, in an unenclosed area. Wild camping is allowed in Scotland under the Land Reform (Scotland) Act 2003, as long as campers leave the site exactly as they found it. This means, with one or two exceptions, that it is possible to camp on the moors, mountains, National Parks and MOD land without landowners' consent. Although good practice is common sense, guidelines are listed at www.outdooraccess-scotland.com

No one in Britain or Ireland lives more than 70 miles from sea.

They include:

- carry a trowel to bury toilet waste
- urinate well away from open water, rivers and burns
- do not overcrowd
- use a stove or leave no trace of any camp fire
- never cut down or damage any tree
- clear all rubbish and litter, even if left by others
- when in doubt, ask the landowner.

Motorhome owners who overnight at non-designated sites usually refer to themselves as 'wild campers'. They typically park anywhere they can: off-road, in lay-bys, on roads or in private or public car parks. The legality of overnight camping on public highways changes from one local authority to another. The best advice is to park late and quietly and move off early, without leaving any trace. Those that like to know their rights, while staying legal, should read the Caravan Sites and Control of Development Act. I was surprised to discover that there is no 'right' to park any vehicle on the road. A tax disc buys the right for the vehicle to be 'driven', not parked.  The legislation does, however, allow hotels, pubs and restaurants to permit a single motorhome or tent to camp overnight in their car park, as long as the area isn't used for camping more than 28 days a year. There are some cracking pubs and hotels by beaches and lakes, so this is a great option. Just book in for an evening meal and camp away for free with the owner's consent. The law also allows local authorities to approve motorhome stopovers on car parks, roads and other land in their control. Some councils allow campers to park right next to the beach. Others don't clarify their position. A list of caravan-friendly councils is listed here: www.motorhomeparking.co.uk

## Staying safe

Apart from the hazards of getting moved on from private or public land while camping wild, the greatest risk involved in camping by water is the wet stuff. The chances of drowning, picking up an infection or colliding with underwater objects are relatively low, but knowing the dangers is essential. I go into more detail on safety in the watersports sections over the following pages but most is common sense: don't go out alone, check tides, ask locals for advice.

Although British waters are considered cleaner than ever, there are still pollution issues, particularly around some parts of Ireland and very occasionally Brighton (work is underway to solve these issues, so check it out). Inland waters carry problems, too. Weill's disease is a bacterial infection picked up on the banks of stagnant and still water by canoeists, fishermen and swimmers. The infection comes mainly from the urine of rodents and farm animals. People can develop flu-like symptoms and think no more about it. Fewer than ten people die from Weill's disease each year in the UK, but awareness is important. The disease is best avoided by covering cuts and abrasions with waterproof dressings, not swallowing still or flowing water and showering after leaving the water.

If this all seems like a lot to remember, don't worry – everything generally falls into place once you pull up at the campsite. Preparation for our family trips mostly involves checking we're legally within the payload at the local weighbridge. Luggage will include rods, inflatable Sevylor canoe, inflatable Henshaw sailing dingy, snorkel, and a passion for bodyboarding. It's close to living the dream. Recently I came across what I think may be the next chapter in our camping odyssey. The Hobie Adventure is a pedal-driven kayak, which comes with paddles, sails, fishing-rod holders and a compartment for diving gear. It's expensive, so I don't think I'll be buying it very soon, but I'm saving hard.

Thanks to all the wardens, campsite owners, fellow travellers and locals who continue to share their knowledge, experience and thoughts. We're still searching for the perfect campsite on water. Some of our favourites are listed here. Enjoy getting out there and discovering them for yourself – the good, the bad and rest.

# getting out on the water

## Camping and sailing

**Ten years ago I bought a second-hand, inflatable sailing dinghy for £600. This Henshaw Tinker Voyager packs into its own bag, the size of a suitcase, which stows inside my motorhome. Rowing with the flood tide is still fun, motoring against it is fine, but nothing beats the exhilaration of hearing a ripple behind the transom as the evening breeze fills her sails.**

There are about 240 coastal marinas in the UK, with tens of thousands of berths. Increased demand over the last 20 years has seen moorings in prime locations diminish as larger vessels have moved in. Many harbour towns remain incredibly beautiful and accessible for boating, but there's a more traditional way to explore the most secluded coastal regions. Adventure sailing involves smaller craft that can cope with rough seas and currents, as well as shallow, inland waters.

Small sailing boats can be launched almost anywhere and carry enough provisions and safety gear for several days away. It's a hobby that is increasingly associated with camping. Escaping the constraints of larger, deep-drafted boats, this sport involves discovering the beauty of narrow estuaries and shallow lagoons that may not have seen a boat in 50 years.

Small craft have been a way of life since ancient times, but the term 'adventure sailing' was coined in the mid-19th century by the middle classes who either bolted make-shift, collapsible rigs onto the side of canoes or adapted shallow-keeled vessels, known as shoal boats. The adventurous Victorians wanted to carry shelter, blankets, warm clothes, food and water for overnight expeditions. The craze faded out as the more proficient sailors craved faster craft and fashion shifted from exploration to speed-racing. A boom in kayaking and canoeing in the last five years is now being followed by a revival in adventure sailing – and it's so much fun. Whether they are yachts, dinghies or kayaks with sails, pocket cruisers are coming back in vogue around Britain's most sheltered creeks and estuaries.

The British coast, if stretched out straight, would almost reach around the circumference of the earth.

My favourite waters for sailing are around the mouth of the River Thames in Essex (where I live, conveniently). The Thames estuary spans an area the shape of a squashed triangle between Essex and Kent, covering hundreds of miles of marshes, creeks, mudflats, inlets, rivers, sandbanks, lagoons and islands. When conditions are good it's a paradise of calm, with endless secret hideaways to pitch a tent among the seabirds, geese, flowers, grasses and seals. My favourite sailing places away from home include the dunes of north-west Wales (Mawddach Estuary, page 96), the clear, turquoise waters of the Outer Hebrides (Isle of Harris, page 66), and the tranquil Camel Estuary in North Cornwall, near Padstow (see page 143). Inland, the Norfolk Broads, the Lake District, and the Scottish and Irish lochs all take some beating. They're the perfect place for campers who want to practise and refine their sailing skills.

By the time you read this, I may have bought a sailing kayak to go with my lightweight bivvy. Thumbing a ride with nature was how they did it in canoes thousands of years ago. And as for the thrill of rediscovering some more of Britain's shallow waters … don't get me started.

There are 19,000 miles of coastline, including the UK's main islands in Britain. Ireland's coastline is estimated at 3,171 miles (Ordnance Survey of Ireland).

**For more information on how to get sailing, contact your local sailing club or try:**
**Open Canoe Sailing Group** www.ocsg.org.uk
**RYA** www.rya.org.uk
**John Floutier Sailing Canoes** www.floutiercanoes.co.uk
**British Marine Federation** www.britishmarine.co.uk

## Safety

These areas are fairly safe, although safety is relative. Courses from local yacht clubs or training centres are the best start. The basics I apply are checking my boat and planning for the worst. Not everything is always possible, but knowing where I've made a compromise helps identify the risks. For me, clothing is crucial. I either wear a good-quality surface dry suit or try to sail the way I surf: expecting to get wet. Check out the section on wetsuits (p.10) and clothing (p.11) for more information. Whatever you decide, base your decisions on first-hand experience and keep learning. Safety isn't complicated or a burden. It's about having the confidence to enjoy.

## Safety checklist

- Assume the craft will malfunction or capsize
- Make sure someone knows your plans (friend, relative, RNLI)
- Carry or wear adequate clothing (wetsuit/surface drysuit or spare clothing in dry bag)
- Have equipment for emergency calls (carry flares/radio/mobile phone)
- Have equipment to help rescuers find you (take a light, flare, whistle or dye)
- Know how to re-float your capsized boat (practise beforehand)
- Know how to make basic repairs (carry a toolbox/replacement parts)
- Carry bungies to tie everything down (bags, fishing rods, paddles, tools)
- Make sure you can survive in the water for as long as possible (wear a fully fitted lifejacket with all the extras, adequate surface drysuit/wetsuit)
- Be aware of your route, including sandbanks, channels and underwater obstructions (carry maps)
- Know how to navigate back in mist, fog or in the dark (take a compass)
- Make sure you can hang onto the boat (attach rope, ties or harness)
- If it is safe, swim back to shore (to do this you will need to be a strong swimmer and have a good knowledge of the tide and the currents)

## Top 10 spots for sailing

### 1 Cardigan Bay

Stay at: **Shell Island Campsite** (p.94)

Cardigan Bay is perfect for yachting. Abersoch, Pwllheli, Portmadoc, Barmouth and Aberdovey are all within a few hours' sail. Boats on trailers need to be registered with Gwynedd, Conwy or Anglesey councils.

### 2 River Ouse

Stay at: **Riverside Campsite** (p.212)

Yachts and dinghies are more popular than ever around the city. York RI Sailing Club is based here and there is a sailing regatta held annually in August.

### 3 Blackwater Estuary

Stay at: **Seaview Holiday Park** (p.176)

Access to the Blackwater Estuary and beyond. West Mersea is one of Essex's most famous sailing spots, with hundreds of river inlets and creeks to explore around the Dengie Peninsula.

### 4  Bristol Channel

Stay at: **Uphill Boat Centre** (p.151)

Good access to the water via this tidal creek. Boats of all sizes can be launched. Members at the adjoining Weston Bay Yacht Club offer good advice. The club has a programme of racing, cruising and social events.

Of the 6000 islands that make up the British Isles, only 140 are inhabited.

### 5  Loch Gairloch and the Atlantic Ocean

Stay at: **Sands Caravan & Camping** (p.70)

Navigate six miles along the loch past the villages of Charlestown, Kerrysdale, Shieldaig, Badachro and Port Henderson. Alternatively, head out along the coast.

### 6  The Atlantic Ocean

Stay at: **Mannix Point Camping & Caravan Park** (p.58)

Home of the Atlantic Sailing Club. Campers can visit the club as long as they come with life jackets and wetsuits. Plenty arrive equipped with their own sailing dinghies and sails.

### 7  Lake Windermere

Stay at: **Hill of Oaks** (p.190)

Restrictions on powered craft have made Windermere more popular than ever. Sailing to Bowness for dinner and drinks is a nice touch.

### 8  Roadford Lake

Stay at: **Roadford Lake Watersports Centre & Camping** (p.145)

A great place to learn. Instructors provide courses for all abilities and there's a resident sailing club.

### 9  Loch Ness

Stay at: **Loch Ness Holiday Park** (p.76)

Who could resist the chance to go Nessie-watching on one of the most famous stretches of water in the world?

### 10 River Thames

Stay at: **Benson Waterfront Riverside Park** (p.134)

The large launch ramp is free for campers. This far inland, and up the Thames, requires a favourable wind and a sense of fun.

The longest river in the UK is the River Severn, stretching 220 miles from Plynlimon in Wales to the Bristol Channel.

# Camping and surfing

I climbed onto a surfboard for the first time at Kuta beach, in Bali, as a 24-year-old. I was a 'seasoned and penniless backpacker' and I thought I knew all about fun. I felt, at the time, that it was a little late in life to take up surfing. Stupid boy! Nothing prepared me for the thrill of skimming fast and wild over water on my belly, atop a 5ft shard of orange and black fibreglass. Twenty-four years later, I still dream about that first wave-ride.

Surfers live on the edge of society to keep the dream alive. In so many ways, campers are doing the same: getting close to nature. That's why, especially among young people, combining the two is so romantic. Visit public car parks after dark around the coastlines of North Devon, Wales and east Scotland and you'll find a small community of nomads known as soul surfers. These wild campers split their time between surfing, free car parks, campsites, meagre work and frugal living. Other than travellers and gypsies, they live closer to nature than almost any social group I can think of. The UK surfing community is bound up with the environmental group SAS, Surfers Against Sewage. It was launched in 1990 by some friends who'd become sick surfing the polluted waters of Cornwall. Two decades on, they are still working hard to eliminate all sewage outfalls around our coastline.

Campsites with great surf are mostly found in Ireland, north Devon, Cornwall, north Wales, the Gower Peninsula (Wales), east Scotland and north-east England. New wetsuit technology means winter swimming or taking the plunge in the coldest summer seas is now easy. There are more details on what gear to wear on pages 10–11.

If dodging breakwaters and camping in the dunes with the cool young dudes doesn't sound like your thing, don't rule out surfing altogether. The sport has always been multi-generational, with old 'soul surfers' camping well into their sixties. It's great for keeping fit and the worse the weather, the better the surf. There are numerous safety organisations and surf schools in the UK offering tuition and free advice for people of all ages and abilities. A cold October day camping in the dunes at the Gower or Cornwall doesn't feel a million miles from that Bali beach – it's still living the dream.

For more information, contact:
**Surf Life Saving GB** www.slsgb.org.uk 01392 218007
**Welsh Surfing Federation Surf School** www.wsfsurfschool.co.uk
**Surfers Against Sewage** www.sas.org.uk

## Safety

Although there's never been a better time to camp 'n' surf on clean beaches, the main danger is turning up unprepared. Colliding with things under the water and drowning are the major risks. Sand bars, jetties and rocks are often hidden. Rip tides around large waves, river estuaries, piers and groynes are usually impossible to see. I've been trapped in these channels and know how difficult it is to stay calm. Many people drown because they panic. The fatal error is trying to swim against the current back to shore. The expert advice is to stay calm, float and wave for help, or swim parallel to the shore, across and out of the channel, (which should be no more than 15 metres wide). Some UK beaches use a colour-code flag system to warn of tidal danger and surfing novices should really only use these beaches. They are zoned:

- **red and yellow** for swimming and bodyboarding
- **black and white** chequered for surfing and kayaking
- **red** for danger (the water should not be entered)

More than 95% of the UK's beaches, rivers and lakes met legal standards of cleanliness in 2011 (European Environment Agency).

# Safety checklist

- Never surf alone
- Seek advice from local surf schools or lifeguards
- If you're in trouble, raise one arm and shout for help
- Do everything you can to stay with your board
- Put your hand and arm over your face and head when resurfacing, to avoid being hit by the surfboard
- Don't swim against a riptide. Instead, float on your back and call for help or swim sideways to the shore, out of the current
- Line yourself up with a landmark to make sure you are not getting pulled too far along the beach by the tides
- Never surf between the red and yellow flags (swimmers only)

Britain's coastline is five times longer than France's, three times longer than Spain's and twice the distance of Italy's.

# Top 10 spots for surfing

**1   Hayle Beach, Celtic Sea**
Stay at: **Sandy Acres** (p.140)
Cornish waves next to a river estuary in the shadow of the Towans. Schools along the beach offer lessons and hire.

**2   Hillend, Bristol Channel**
Stay at: **Hillend Caravan & Camping Park** (p.101)
The best water on the Gower Peninsula. The Welsh Surfing Federation operates tuition for beginners and intermediates.

**3   Banff Links, the North Sea**
Stay at: **Banff Links Caravan Park** (p.78)
This north-facing strip attracts boarders from all over Scotland. Good at any time of the day, but best between low- and mid-tide. Careful of the rocks.

**4   Cardigan Bay, the Irish Sea**
Stay at: **Cae Du Campsite** (p.97)
Better two hours either side of the tide. Catch glimpses of dolphins at dawn and dusk.

**5   Ashington, The North Sea**
Stay at: **Sand Bay Holiday Park** (p.203)
Boarders ride the waves either side of River Wansbeck, direct from the campsite. The surf can whip up here, so take care around the rocks.

**6   Skegness Sands, the North Sea**
Stay at: **Skegness Sands Touring Site** (p.221)
One of two main surf areas in Lincolnshire (the other is Sandilands at Sutton-on-Sea). There are waves all year, although autumn is best. The Lincolnshire Surf Club, established in 2006, offers good advice.

**7   Brighstone Bay, the English Channel**
Stay at: **Grange Farm** (p.163)
This exposed section of the English Channel makes it one of the finest beaches on the south coast. There are more reef breaks further along the coast between the Chines, too.

**8   Fraserburgh, the North Sea**
Stay at: **Fraserburgh Esplanade Caravan Park** (p.79)
Kitesurfing has become big business here. The east-facing shore provides consistently good waves all year round. Spring is best but autumn is kinder for rookies.

**9   Brean, River Severn Estuary**
Stay at: **Channel View** (p.150)
Better than Weston-super-Mare as the surf is bigger, and there's usually less wind thanks to the landscape. The beach is good for windsurfing.

**10 Lettergesh, the Atlantic Ocean**
Stay at: **Connemara Caravan & Camping Park** (p.50)
A gentle introduction to the best region in Ireland and Britain for rookie boarders. In County Clare, to the south, the Cliffs of Moher attract thousands of visitors each year and many want to either see or ride Aileen's, Ireland's biggest wave.

The CIA World Factbook ranks Britain's coast as the 12th longest in the world.

# Camping and fishing

**If camping has a first cousin, this is it. There are about five million anglers and two million campers in Britain and Ireland. Aside from sleeping, fishing is the most peaceful thing I do. I enter a dreamy state of wakefulness, until a tiny creature with baffling strength tugs and bends my rod. Homemade rods, a few pounds worth of hooks and floats and earthworms, and a little knowledge are all that's needed to feel the thrill of a tight line. Failing to catch dents the desire to return. Freshwater fisheries with their own campsites are the best place to learn because owners have a vested interest in your success – happy campers always come back.**

Every county in Britain and Ireland has more than one campsite with on-site fishing. Most have tackle shops manned by staff who want to pass on good advice. Training schools for kids cost almost nothing.  If you're in need of angling tips, the four basic rules I apply are:

1 Find a fishery or campsite with a reputation for good, plentiful stock
2 Ask for guidance on baits, tackle and water depth
3 Tackle up with the precision of a surgeon. You can learn in 20 minutes by watching YouTube or reading a book
4 Place groundbait in the exact area you've decided to fish

England has thousands of lakes – 389 of them are over 12 acres in size.

There are two angling zones associated with camping: freshwater (coarse) and seawater, and thousands of methods (I've yet to perfect any of them). My sea-fishing expeditions are attempts to bring something home to cook on the campfire. Coarse fishing (freshwater lakes, rivers and canals) rarely involves any thoughts of dinner. Encounters inland with beautiful creatures, festooned in fine scales and extra-terrestrial colours almost always involve 'catch and release'. It's a perplexing idea to some, but routine practice at private fisheries, controlled by regulations. Salmon and trout are the exceptions. Game fishing – either in sea or freshwater – involves casting man-made flies into the watery void. It's more art than science. Many game anglers will keep what they catch, but increasingly they are choosing to release, too.

If fish don't bite, experiment. It's great fun watching everyone else missing with the spam and pellets, while you're hooking six-pound carp and bream on bread flakes or red foil paper. You'll be amazed at what a fish will try to eat on any given day. Your chosen location around the water is important, too. When I'm looking for a campsite and fishery, I tend to book a site where the area I intend to fish (known as a swim) is included within the pitch area. There's something special about having everything within easy reach, especially a gas hob and fridge. The downside is if your swim is producing no bites, it's not so easy to move. Some fisheries set the campsite a few hundred yards from the water so anglers can move about, if necessary, between swims.

Sea fishing is a completely different discipline. As I can't afford a 'fishing boat', the method I use is line-fishing from a kayak. Kayak fishing is one of the fastest-growing sports in the UK and Ireland. Its success is based around the ability to reach the very best fishing grounds, inaccessible to other craft. Clubs and associations offer information on where to fish, how to improve the chances of success, and how to stay safe.

Campsites on coasts, estuaries, sea lochs and tidal rivers are rarely designed to cater for anglers. It's more about going it alone or looking for advice from others. There are literally thousands of campsites with exclusive access to ponds, rivers, lakes, canals and beaches that others can't reach.

I've fly-fished for trout on the River Eden in north-west England (p.182), watched my daughter hook eight-pound carp at Bosworth Water Trust, in Nuneaton (p.116) and caught cod and mackerel on a handline from a kayak along the west coast of Scotland (p.74). The islands off the Scottish coast

More than 10% of holiday parks and campsites are open all year.

and the Welsh shoreline around Snowdonia are, for me, the best sea-fishing, and the south-west coast of Ireland isn't far behind. The entire British coast can be successfully fished, although inland is my favourite zone for relaxation: casting a line onto a still lake, next to camp, is a fairy-tale world. Five million anglers and two million campers can't be wrong.

For more advice on where and how to catch fish, safety and how to buy a freshwater license see:
**The Environment Agency** www.environment-agency.gov.uk
**Waterscape** www.waterscape.com/things-to-do/angling
**The Angling Trust** www.anglingtrust.net
**Anglers' Net** www.anglersnet.co.uk
**www.Fish-uk.com**
**Talk Angling UK** www.talkangling.co.uk,
**Fish Talk Ireland** www.fishingtalkireland.com
**The Irish Federation of Pike Angling Clubs** www.angling-in-ireland.com

*There are 31,460 freshwater lochs in Scotland.*

For more on sea-fishing:
**World Sea Fishing** www.worldseafishing.com (with 40,000 online members)
**www.sea-fishing.org** (with almost 11,000 online members)

For kayak fishing:
**Kayak Fishing UK** www.kayakfishinguk.net
**Anglers Afloat** www.anglersafloat.co.uk
**South Wales Kayak Anglers** www.SWKA.org.uk

## Safety

Some of the risks involved in fishing and boating offshore are outlined in the kayaking and sailing sections (pp.21 and 36). Most fatalities in angling occur when people fall overboard or stumble from rocks while sea-fishing. When inland, focus first on looking for overhead power cables. Carbon-fibre fishing rods conduct electricity and they don't even have to touch the power cables to prove fatal. Electricity can arc (jump) from a power line to a rod and a five-metre arc is possible from one of the highest-voltage power lines (400 kV). The minimum height for a 400kV power line in the UK is seven metres, well within the danger range if you're carrying a six-metre rod.

# Top 10 spots for fishing

1    River Eden
Stay at: **Lazonby Campsite** (p.182)
Campers are permitted to fly-fish from next to a public footpath that runs along the riverbank. The trout feed on the mayflies during late summer.

2    Lakeside Lake
Stay at: **Lakeside Adults-Only Touring Caravan Park** (p.215)
A six-acre lake, set up as a mixed-course fishery, open for angling from 7 am until 9 pm or dusk, for a day-entry fee. Ground bait by feeder only.

**3  Loch Eil**

Stay at: **Linnhe Lochside Holidays** (p.75)

Rods and tackle are available for hire or sale from the camp shop. Angling is free. Pike and trout fishing are the favourites. Mackerel feed off the pier next to the Caledonian Canal, a five-minute drive away.

**4  River Great Ouse**

Stay at: **St Neots Camping & Caravanning Club** (p.234)

This river is brimming over with fish. Carp regularly come in at 20lb. Bait up with bread flakes, luncheon meat, sweetcorn and red maggots from the village.

**5  River Wyre and the Irish Sea**

Stay at: **Morfa Farm Caravan Park** (p.100)

Trout fishing on three-quarters of a mile of river. Fish offshore at the front of the site for whiting, flatfish and mackerel.

**6  River Slaney**

Stay at: **Ferrybank Caravan & Camping** (p.54)

Purported to be one of the best fishing rivers in Ireland. There are sea trout and salmon upstream; mullet, garfish and flounder close to camp.

**7  River Wenning**

Stay at: **Riverside Caravan Park** (p.191)

There's a run of salmon and sea trout from the end of July to the close of the season. The site owners have the fishing rights to the Wenning for about a mile on either side, and are involved in a trout-stocking programme. An on-site lake is stocked with carp, rudd, roach and perch.

**8  Sumners Ponds**

Stay at: **Sumners Ponds** (p.168)

The lakes are stocked with large carp, pike and easy-to-catch silverfish. The resident water bailiff offers good advice and provides bait and tackle in the campsite café and shop.

**9  River Stour**

Stay at: **Meadowbank Holidays** (p.156)

Large barbel, chub and pike are caught here. During the summer, mullet swim upstream from Christchurch. Float fishing with hemp and tares is good for roach. Bread flake or cheese paste work for chub. Maggots and casters are better for barbel.

**10 Winchcombe Lake**

Stay at: **Winchcombe Camping & Caravanning Club Site** (p.128)

Catch carp and chub from wooden swims around the edge of the lake. Spam works best. Maggots are banned.

The UK's largest lake is Lough Neagh, in Northern Ireland (18 x 9 miles).

# Camping and wild swimming

**Swimming outdoors is like being reborn. You enter the water with a shiver, feeling vulnerable but you come out refreshed and alive. I learnt to swim on the River Thames. Frantic strokes, head down, not coming up for air, throwing right arm after left again and again, quicker and faster, before surfacing, crowned in seaweed, chin dripping, and a mouth full of Thames mud – but very excited.**

Whether it's a murky river, a crystal-cool lake or a bay of surf, wild swimming fires the senses into life at once. The body is suspended in space, the brain switches to high alert, the skin tingles. All the while, the natural world – the water, the sky, and the land – is wrapped about us and we seem tiny in comparison. The late Roger Deakin describes it beautifully in *Waterlog: A Swimmer's Journey Through Britain*. The journalist Kate Rew (author of *Wild Swim*) founded the excellent Outdoor Swimming Society in 2006. But for all the media interest, most inland waters seem to me as deserted as ever. I think there are three reasons for this: the coldness of the water, self-consciousness about our bodies and a fear of the unknown.

The first and second can be overcome together. Buy a good wetsuit and slip inside. When you get too warm, take the wetsuit off. It feels less daunting once you're in. Inhibitions soon disappear and the suit is less and less necessary. The best swimwear is a triathlete suit, which can easily be hired out for a season for a few pounds. It offers a good combination of warmth and freedom of movement. So wetsuits resolve self-consciousness and the problem of the cold water. I think the cold is party linked to the last issue, too: fear. Losing heat in the water can be dangerous. The body's extremities shut down, your blood moves to protect your organs and limbs lose their movement. Even venturing just a few yards into the chilliest water can make getting back to shore difficult. Without help, cold swimmers in trouble can drown. Tides and currents are another concern. Always ask locals and never swim without taking advice. The unknown can relate to water quality, too. There are risks (especially around still water where rodent and farm animal urine can cause Weill's disease), although the UK waters are the cleanest they've ever been. The Environment Agency website provides a helpful interactive map, with cleanliness ranked from A–F (A is very clean) for chemistry and biology or 1–6 (1 is very low) for nitrates or phosphates.

For the very adventurous, coasteering is increasing in popularity. Coasteering is a combination of swimming and rock climbing that involves exploring the join between land and sea, while discovering caves and jumping into seawater pools that have been assessed as safe. It's not for me, but there are plenty of good, professional guide groups around the country, especially around south-west England, Wales, Ireland and Scotland.

The longest canal in the UK is the Grand Union Canal, stretching 137 miles from Birmingham to London.

Inland, some of my favourite swims are from campsites in the Norfolk Broads, the River Stour in Suffolk, Loch Lomond and Windermere. Camping can remove a lot of inhibitions about slipping into the water. Once you are pitched by the river, lake or lagoon, the first thing to do is explore – especially if you're in a canoe or boat. Taking the plunge after a sweaty and wet river journey is the most natural thing to do. Try it.

**Very good information on safety and swimming locations is available from:**
**The Outdoor Swimming Society** www.outdoorswimmingsociety.com
**The River and Lake Swimming Association** www.river-swimming.co.uk

Wales
has more
than 220
large lakes.

# Top 10 spots for wild swimming

### 1   River Camel / Little Petherick Creek

Stay at: **Trevitha Farm** (p.143)

I wanted to put this in the canoe section because it is possible to paddle from Trevitha Farm to Padstow for evening drinks, but clear-water swimming always trumps boats in my book. This is probably the most wonderful stretch of creek in Britain.

### 2   Chichester Harbour

Stay at: **Fishery Creek Caravan & Camping Park** (p.165)

Of all the things to do, lazing about in this warm creek watching canoeists and sailors launch around high tide is about as pleasurable as life gets.

### 3   Loch Lomond

Stay at: **Luss Camping & Caravanning Club Site** (p.81)

The water is at its warmest in September, when it's possible to ditch the wetsuit. The loch is clear enough to snorkel.

### 4   River Frome

Stay at: **Stowford Manor Farm** (p.153)

A treasure. Farleigh & District Swimming Club is 200 metres away and claims to be the only river club in the country. Founded in 1933, it has more than 2,000 members who use the deeper part of the river above the weir.

### 5   River Waveney

Stay at: **Outney Meadow Caravan Park** (p.229)

Clean and shallow, and kids love making a splash from the tree swings.

### 6   Atlantic Ocean

Stay at: **Horgabost Camping** (p.66)

A beach with a view over to Taransay Island (of BBC *Castaway* fame). A spectacular coast, bordered to the left side by a creek for jumping about in.

### 7   River Stour
Stay at: **Rushbanks Farm** (p.237)
Campers come here to bathe and canoe. Everyone gets along just fine – even the ducks.

### 8   River Dwyryd
Stay at: **Llechrwd Farm** (p.91)
Camping beside a shallow, fast-flowing river that travels from Snowdonia to the Irish Sea. The furthest field from the entrance contains a deep-water hole.

### 9   Gosfield Lake
Stay at: **Gosfield Lake Resort** (p.173)
Triathletes come here to train, and open-water swims are held too. The times of these are published at reception and online.

### 10 Atlantic Ocean
Stay at: **The Croft Caravan & Campsite** (p.74)
A clean, safe bay, warmed by the Gulf Stream. When the tide goes out there are deep rock pools and creeks to wallow about in while watching the weather come in on the horizon..

There are more than 600 rivers and canals in Britain and Ireland, spread across 7,000 miles.

# Camping, canoeing and kayaking

**Canoeing was the UK's fastest growing watersport in 2012. Although canoe-camping is more popular in North America, small boats epitomise the freedom associated with traditional camping on this side of the water. That's why combining the two makes such perfect sense. Caravans and tents give us the opportunity to explore Britain's rural landscape but paddle-power is the true vehicle of discovery, catapulting the traveller from the safety of the campsite into the unknown.**

The experience is both exhilarating and hazardous. Nowadays, only the daft few leave the shore without lifejackets, but many still paddle unprepared, forgetting to check tides or take adequate clothing. It's worth remembering that cold water – even in late spring – can shock a person into hypothermia or gulp reflex (inhaling water involuntarily due to cold). One warm day in April, I put a canoe on the River Thames from a wild camping site at Two Tree Island, in Essex (p.158). Leaving the mouth of the estuary, I paddled alone for two hours towards London against the outgoing tide, intending to drift back on the low tide from Thurrock, trailing spinners to catch bass. I turned for home at five o'clock, but within 10 minutes the wind had blown against the current, creating choppy waters and no way back. As the sun slipped behind the horizon, the new tide was only 30 minutes from turning against me, too. I was incredibly cold, miles away from any help, my mobile phone was out of battery, and I had only light clothing. Luckily, the wind eventually dropped and I managed to paddle far enough back to get to a road where I phoned for a pick-up. This is a lesson in why it is essential to always plan and prepare.

Canoes carry more than any backpack can, which means there was no good reason for me to be unprepared. Experienced canoeists exploit this ability to stock up and choose to camp under or inside their craft, with a tarpaulin throw-over shelter, a pot for cooking on an open fire (or camping stove), a healthy food store, water and warm, waterproof clothing.

Kayaks are attracting a new breed of adventurer who wants to combine fishing with exploring some of Britain's most rugged coastline. Canoes may be the connoisseurs of calm on rivers and inland lakes but kayaks are sleek sea creatures designed to glide over the roughest waves, enabling the pilot to surf, roll and ride. Kayaks can cut through currents and wind that traditional rowing boats and canoes have no hope of coping with. Their narrow hulls mean kayakers must master the art of rolling in order to enjoy the open seas without fear of capsizing.

Inland, the boundaries are only restricted by access to water and the location of campsites. Among the best rivers with good access are the Wye and Severn, which span both England and Wales. The River Waveney and the Broads in Suffolk and Norfolk are outstanding. The coasts of Ireland and Scotland, particularly around the Hebrides, are best for kayaks – both offering some of the clearest and finest fishing waters in the UK.

Membership of the British Canoe Union grants access to 2800 miles of British waterways, without the need to buy individual permits for rivers and canals. Once you have a permit, wild camping is the most wonderful way to navigate water where no official sites exist, although wild canoe camping is best suited to Scotland, where legislation allows unlimited access. The archaic public access laws of England, Ireland and Wales are still in need of change.

There's almost no limit to the regions and tidal waterways that remain largely unexplored by these simple craft. Narrow boats transport us from Earth as we know it, into an amazing world of reed beds, mudflats, seaweed, giant insects, and wildlife. It's a cheap, family sport that will continue to grow – alongside camping – as a great outdoor adventure.

Birmingham has one hundred miles of canal, more than Venice.

For more information on canoeing:

**Song of the Paddle** www.songofthepaddle.co.uk

**British Canoe Union**, the national body for canoeing. www.bcu.org.uk

**The Camping and Caravanning Club** has its own Canoe-Camping Club which produces monthly magazines, holds rallies and offers safety advice. www.canoecampingclub.co.uk

**Sea Kayaking UK** provides information on training courses put on by the BCU and others. www.seakayakinguk.com/courses

## Safety

The main things to remember are:

- don't canoe alone.
- carry flares and whistles to call for help.
- never set out without a lifejacket.
- wear or carry adequate clothing in winter and summer (choices include surface drysuit, wetsuit or spare dry clothes).
- check tides and winds.
- carry a phone that is well charged.

# Top 10 spots for canoeing/kayaking

### 1 River Wye

Stay at: **Lucksall Touring & Camping Park** (p.123)

Canadian canoes for hire here – especially good for those who want to take advantage of pick-up points along the river. Drivers will carry you back to camp. Two launches, either end of the site.

### 2 Derwentwater

Stay at: **Keswick Camping & Caravanning Site** (p.185)

Great for exploring hidden coves and the islands, against a backdrop of impressive skies and vast peaks.

### 3 River Mawddach

Stay at: **Fegla Fach Farm Caravan Club CL** (p.96)

This river estuary has many areas to explore that only a narrow craft can navigate. Ideal for line-fishing from your own boat.

### 4 River Ure

Stay at: **Sleningford Watermill** (p.206)

The Ure is rated a Grade 2/3-white water along this section, providing a challenge for paddlers at all levels. River access is free for campers. Boat hire is available.

### 5 River Ouse

Stay at: **Linton Lock Marina & Campsite** (p.209)

More experienced canoeists take on the salmon leap. Pay a small fee to launch your own canoe.

## 6  Atlantic Ocean

Stay at: **Traigh Na Beirigh** (p.64)

Don't arrive at the best campsite in Scotland without being able to navigate your way around the shallows. The surrounding islands have the most beautiful hidden beaches and bays. Offshore fishing from a canoe or kayak is good, too.

## 7  River Severn

Stay at: **Severn House Campsite** (p.113)

People camp overnight as part of their river-tour expeditions. Launching is free for resident campers.

## 8  River Thames

Stay at: **Chertsey Camping & Caravanning Club Site** (p.167)

It's easy to launch a canoe along the entire east side of the site. The park hosts canoe-camping events throughout the year.

## 9  River Waveney

Stay at: **Rowan Craft Caravan Club Site** (p.230)

Beccles is about a three-hour paddle from this section of the Suffolk Broads. A low bridge prevents larger vessels entering the water system. There are lots of boats available to hire.

## 10 Avonmore River

Stay at: **Hidden Valley Holiday Park** (p.53)

Guided tours through the Avonmore Valley are available. Hire boats or bring your own.

# part 2
## regional guides

# ireland

I defy anyone to arrive in Ireland's slow lane without feeling a sense of homecoming. Deserted roads lazily trail through a bygone era of log fires, empty beaches, loughs, surf and riverbank. This is Europe's most unexplored region. If Africa is the cradle of civilisation, Ireland is the crèche that nurtured it. But few people get beyond the Hollywood clichés, chatshow hosts and church-inspired sitcoms, and actually see the Irish in their homeland. That's partly thanks to overpriced campsites and shockingly expensive ferries. Thankfully, times are changing.

The Republic makes up most of the island. The smaller UK region, in the north, is beautiful and more affordable. The Troubles continue to hurt both sides of the divide. Politics rarely get in the way for travellers, but Ireland is like anywhere else in that sense – it pays to be cautious. Caution should also extend to the relative calmness of the traffic – take care on the roads. A four-week tour will give you plenty of time to discover this island without rushing and there's no shortage of activities wherever you are. Good clothing is essential – the west coast can see some of the heaviest rainfall in northern Europe. Camping in Ireland is commonly seen as being less about discovering the 'real Ireland' (it's never hidden) and all about finding the real value.

The west side is the most spectacular, with the Lakes of Killarney, the Dingle Peninsula, Connemara and the Aran Islands. Croaghaun is one of the world's highest sea cliffs. The Cliffs of Moher are unforgettable. The Aileens are famous for humpback whales, movie backdrops and the biggest, most dangerous surfing wave in Europe. Tow-surfers and bodyboarders only conquered its breathtaking breaks in recent years. Mullaghmore and Pampa are great for surfing, too.

For freshwater angling, Lough Currane is the main water in a catchment of six lakes between the mountains and western Atlantic seashore. The Upper Waterville Lakes offer excellent brown-trout, sea-trout and salmon fishing. Ballina, in County Mayo, is the salmon capital of Ireland and an important base for game fishing. The Moy system can produce well over 12,000 rod-caught salmon in a season.

On the east coast, the village of Kilmore Quay, in south Wexford, makes claim to fierce bass, huge pollack, thrashing tope and blue shark. Further along the coast road is Waterford, the city my family came from three generations ago. From here, beaches trail down to Cork, Kinsale and Clonakilty, with some of the best sands at Inchydoney and Owenahincha. West Cork and Kerry are home to five peninsulas that jut out into the Atlantic, endless harbours, bays and islands. Beyond Clonakilty, the coast road weaves its way to Baltimore, Lough Hyne and Bantry.

Six million people live in southern and northern Ireland, compared to 60 million on the UK mainland (not including Northern Ireland). Almost 25 per cent of the UK population claim to have Irish roots. Yet Brits account for only 30 per cent of the foreign market in Ireland and the ferry prices go a long way to explaining why: the shortest routes cost a minimum of £400 return during the summer months. Quieter ferry routes, from Ireland to France, are much cheaper. The good news is that the Irish government is desperate to boost the failing economy and there are moves to address

the 'ferry issue' by bringing together the boat companies and camping organisations to find a solution. Fáilte Ireland, the country's tourist development agency, completed a strategic review of the Irish Caravan and Camping Sector in 2011 and admitted there were problems that needed resolving.

The price of campsites, food and provisions in the Republic is high. Expect to pay the equivalent of £35 per night, with lots of extras on top (north of the border, prices can be 25 per cent cheaper). Some of the very best campsites are listed over the following pages. Seasoned campers often choose to combine paid-for sites with wild camping and pub car park stopovers during a trip and councils are slowly beginning to reconsider the near-blanket ban on overnighting in public car parks. Several councils are even looking to adopt the French aires-de-service system (a network of stopover points for caravans and motorhomes). Until this happens, overnighting in pub car parks is a good option. Excellent value meals are served at lunchtime (avoid evenings, when food is double the price) and many landlords and owners outside of the major towns are happy to allow the odd motorhome, caravan or tent in the car park on condition of a modest spend in the bar. The Irish outback is so beautiful that any chance to go wild around its outer extremities, within the law, should be taken. Wild camping isn't legal (as it is in Scotland), but it's sometimes permitted in some of the most remote areas if codes of conduct are observed (see, for example, www.wicklowmountainsnationalpark.ie/WildCamping).

County Mayo, Sligo, Donegal and Connemara are especially good. I've rarely experienced problems and am overcome at times by the warm welcome. They call it Irish charm, but there's rarely a hint of self-interest; just people who offer practical altruism, dry wit, mañana and a child-like enthusiasm for kindness. Home from home.

ATLANTIC OCEAN
N
Tory Island
Tory Sound
Sheep Haven
Bloody Foreland
N56
Aran Island
Crohy Head
Dungloe
Letterkenny
Gweebarra Bay
N13
Ballybofey
Rossan Point
Ardara
N15
N56
Donegal
Lough Derg
Donegal Bay
Ballyshannon
Benwee Head
A46
N15
Lough Melvin
Sligo Bay
Sligo
N16
A4
The Mullet
N59
N59
Ballina
N17
N4
Lough Gill
Lough Allen
Lough Conn
Achill Head
Achill Island
Shannon Erne
N5
Boyle
Carrick -on-Shan
2
Clare Island
Clew Bay
Castlebar
Westport
N84
N17
N61
Lough Boderg
N60
N5
Inishbofin
N59
Lough Mask
Longfo
Roscommon
N63
N83
Lough Ree
Tuam
N59
N63
N61
Lough Corrib
Athlone
N17
M6
Ballinasloe
Kilkieran Bay
3
Galway
M6
Galway Bay
Loughrea
N65
Inishmore
Aran Islands
N66
N52
N67
Gort
Slieve Bl
Mounta
Cliffs of Moher
Lough Derg
Roscrea
N85
M18
N52
M7
N7
Ennis
Nenagh
N68
N62
Shannon
Limerick
Slievefelim Mountains
Kilrush
N69
Loop Head
Mouth of the Shannon
N24
Tipperary
N21
N20
Tralee Bay
N69
Brandon Head
Clonmel
Tralee
M8
N76
Castleisland
Mitchelstown
N86
N73
Mallow
Killarney
N72
Blackwater
N72
N72
Dingle Bay
N70
Lough Leane
Valencia Island
8
N22
N70
Cork
Midleton
N25
N71
Bolus Head
Kenmare River
Cork Harbour
Knockadoon Head
6
N71
7
Bantry Bay
Clonakilty
N71
Mizen Head
Cape Clear
Galley Head

# Cranfield Caravan Park ①
123 Cranfield Road, Kilkeel, County Down, BT34 4LJ

**Cranfield Caravan Park sits on Carlingford Lough, close to where it feeds into the Irish Sea and the Cooley Mountains rise up from the horizon. The views over the beach at dawn on a cloudless day are incredible. Cranfield Point is the most southerly point of Northern Ireland – the middle of the lough forms the boundary between Northern Ireland and the Republic of Ireland, its northern shores in County Down and the southern side in County Louth.**

Cranfield Bay is for surfers, windsurfers, anglers and sailors. A boat launch is within a few minutes of the campsite (apply to Warrenpoint Tourist Office for use). Canoes and kayaks can be put in the water directly from the site. The currents around the flood and ebb tides are strong so care is needed, particularly around the mouth of the lough. It's a two-mile paddle to the other side, which is too far for me. The edges are relatively shallow, with mudflats and occasional creeks that are worth exploring. Rivers running into the lough rise in the Mourne Mountains of County Down, the Cooley Mountains of County Louth and Slieve Gullion in County Armagh. Heading north-west in a canoe along the shore towards the Norman castle of Greencastle is best. Green Island is opposite the castle and excellent for bird watching. The lough narrows at Warrenpoint, a small town at the most northerly point of the shore. Canoeists can get in and out at the old stone quay on the Newry side of the castle. Good places to fish are either along the shore or float fishing from rocks. Cod, mackerel, bass, flounder, rays and dogfish are most common. The lough is renowned for tope fishing and charter boats are available. Mackerel are caught from either shore or boat. Bass and sea trout are taken on lures, sand eels or fly.

Forty pitches are towards the park entrance next to the beach, opposite Haulbowline Lighthouse. Most are hard-standing and come with electrical hook-up, wastewater point and TV outlet. Toilets and showers are very clean. Tents aren't catered for. Warrenpoint is about a 20-minute drive away. Resort towns of Warrenpoint and Rostrevor lie on the County Down shore. The Cooley Peninsula, on the other side of the lough, is home to the coastal towns of Omeath and Carlingford.

BEST IN
County Down

# site info

**OPEN** March to October

**DIRECTIONS** Exit the A2 at Kilkeel and follow signs for the campsite, which is reached within 10 minutes.

**YEP** Dogs, showers, toilets, caravans, motorhomes, electric

**NO** Tents, shop, bar, restaurant, play area, equipment hire

**ACTIVITIES** Canoe, kayak, fish, swim, snorkel, sailing dinghy, surf

**RATING** Facilities ★★★★★ Location ★★★★★ Water activities ★★★★★

02841 762572

www.cranfieldcaravanpark.co.uk

# Connemara Caravan & Camping Park ❷
## Gowlaun, Lettergesh, Renvyle, County Galway

**White sands and clear waters at Lettergesh don't attract the thousands of visitors they get further south, which is why I like it here. Twelve Bens Mountains form the backdrop, with views over the Mayo Mountains. Nearby Renvyle peninsula is close to being Europe's most westerly point. Discovering the beauty spots (Derryinver Quay, Ballinakill Harbour) alone and in your own time is a fun way to pass the days off-site, in between dolphin watching, relaxing and canoeing.**

Kayaking is superb, but care is needed if venturing too far around the coast. Fishing from a kayak just off the beach is good, too. From the shore, turbot and flounder are most commonly caught. Good advice is available from Duffy's Tackle Shop in Galway. Surfing the waves along this entire stretch of coast is excellent, although the campsite is protected and only surfs well when the wind is from the west or north. It rains a lot, so a good wetsuit is essential to avoid wind chill. In winter it's not uncommon to see surfers wearing six-millimetre suits. The winds make for excellent windsurfing and sailing, although access to the beach is via steps, which can cause problems if you're carrying heavy gear.

The campsite has 40 pitches open from May to September, with electricity. Pitch either high or low, depending on how confident you are that your camp set-up can cope with the winds. Facilities include showers, toilets and a laundry room. Tully Cross has several good pubs. If heading inland, Killary Adventure Centre offers a programme of sports to test your skill. Lough Fee and Lough Muc are well worth exploring.

*BEST IN*
*County*
*Galway*

## site info

**OPEN** May to September

**DIRECTIONS** Leave the N59 8 miles north east of Clifden. Head towards Tully Cross and then follow the signs for Gowlaun. Campsite is next to the beach.

**YEP** Dogs, showers, toilets, tents, caravans, motorhomes, electric, play area,

**NO** Shop, bar, restaurant, equipment hire

**ACTIVITIES** Canoe, kayak, fish, swim, surf

**RATING** Facilities ★★★★★ Location ★★★★★
Water activities ★★★★★

+00 353 (0) 9543406

www.connemaracaravans.com

# Salthill Caravan Park  ③
## Salthill, Galway City

**Campers come here for peaceful seclusion, within walking distance of Galway City. Salthill is bordered on three sides by Galway Bay. To the west, at the mouth of the bay, are the three Aran Islands: Inis Mór Island (Big Island), Inis Meáin Island (Middle Island) and Inis Oírr Island (East Island). Galway itself sits on the River Corrib, with its network of canals and channels.**

The bay is protected from the prevailing winds, which makes for good fishing on the open water. Tope and large rays are caught off shore, particularly around the south-east beach areas of Newquay. If hiring a motorboat, the islands are supposed to be the best fishing. Kayak fishing is popular here, too. Galway Kayak Club offers advice to anyone launching on the bay. Canals around Galway are a safe introduction for rookie paddlers, with access to the River Corrib towards Lough Corrib. Surfing is only possible when the winds blow onshore. Take advice before swimming.

Most of the 70 pitches have great views in all directions of the Burren and the Clare Hills. Facilities include showers, toilets, children's playroom, laundry room and undercover eating area. A pub, shop and supermarket are nearby. Buses pass the campsite gate every 30 minutes. Galway can be reached from the campsite via a coastal pathway, which passes by the seaside village of Salthill, less than a mile away.

## site info

**OPEN** April to September

**DIRECTIONS** From Sligo pass Galway city onto N6, past all roundabouts until Deane Roundabout. After 300 metres turn right onto the R337. Continue straight and then next left at Joyces' supermarket, and right after 20 metres.

**YEP** Dogs, showers, toilets, tents, caravans, motorhomes, play area, electric

**NO** Shop, bar, restaurant, equipment hire

**ACTIVITIES** Canoe, kayak, fish, swim, snorkel, sailing dinghy, surf

**RATING** Facilities ★★★★★ Location ★★★★★ Water activities ★★★★★

+00 353 (0) 91 523972

www.salthillcaravanpark.com

# Hidden Valley Holiday Park 4
## Rathdrum, County Wicklow

**Hidden Valley is a chance to savour life under a forest canopy, within walking distance of civilisation. The Avonmore River flows through the Vale of Clara – a beautiful valley setting that could have been crafted for canoes. Avondale Forest Park to the south and Wicklow Mountains National Park to the north are less than 10 miles from the camp. Rathdrum's restaurants and shops are 10 minutes away.**

The river dominates the park. It joins the Avonbeg, a few miles south of Avondale, at the Meeting of the Waters to form the River Avoca, before it flows into the Irish Sea. Kayaks and rowing boats can be hired out for either the campsite lake or the river. Guided canoe tours are available. The Avonmore holds large stocks of wild brown trout. Fishing with permits is allowed either on site or from forest trails along the riverbank. The best times are spring (March–May) and early autumn (late August–September). Swimming is good, with shallow pools for paddling or deeper areas for inflatables and rafts. There's a beach area for kids.

Several pitches are positioned around the boating lake. Toilets and showers are clean and modern. The laundry room and kitchen overlook the Avonmore. BBQs are available from reception. Campfires are allowed riverside.

**BEST IN County Wicklow**

## site info

**OPEN** April to September

**DIRECTIONS** Turn off the R752 half a mile north of Rathdrum and follow the signs for Hidden Valley.

**YEP** Dogs, showers, toilets, tents, caravans, motorhomes, electric, equipment hire, games room

**NO** Shop, bar, restaurant

**ACTIVITIES** Canoe, kayak, fish, swim

**RATING** Facilities ★★★★★ Location ★★★★★ Water activities ★★★★★

+00 353 (0) 86 7272 872

www.hiddenvalleypark.ie

# Ferrybank Caravan & Camping **5**
Ferrybank, Wexford

**Council-run sites don't get better than this. Ferrybank comes with its own swimming pool and gym, and it overlooks Wexford Harbour. Best of all, it has direct access to one of the most fish-rich rivers in Ireland. The town lies on the south side of Wexford Harbour, on the estuary of the River Slaney. It was once a major port, until the deep-water Rosslare Harbour was created 12 miles south. Fishing boats and pleasure craft still use the harbour at Wexford.**

Boating and kayaking from the campsite are excellent. A series of steps leads down from the campsite to the edge of a vast expanse of natural harbour and the River Slaney estuary. From here it's possible to fish and explore, either carrying on out into the Atlantic or heading upstream on the Slaney. Sailing from Wexford to Enniscorthy is 12 miles upriver. Launching directly from the campsite is difficult for anything other than a small dinghy craft that can be manually carried. Anglers claim this section of river is one of the best in Ireland. Large numbers of sea trout and salmon can be fished well upstream. Bass and eels are around the mid-sections. Mullet, garfish and flounder are in the lower reaches, close to camp.  As a very general rule, worms, small spinners, lures and flies work best upstream, and sand eels, ragworm and lugworm closer to the estuary.

The campsite is just over the bridge that spans the Slaney, within easy walking distance of the town. Almost 100 pitches are spread about the 10-acre site. Toilets and shower blocks are good and clean. Superb facilities include a 25-metre swimming pool, sauna, steam room and first-floor gym, with panoramic views of the Wexford Estuary.  Although it's open to the public, campers get concessions. The campsite has easy access to the main N11 and N25 roads. Sandy beaches along the Wexford coast are nearby.

## site info

**OPEN** May to September

**DIRECTIONS** Just a mile and a half east of Wexford town, across the bridge, on the R741.

**YEP** Dogs, showers, toilets, tents, caravans, motorhomes, play area, electric

**NO** Shop, bar, restaurant, equipment hire

**ACTIVITIES** Canoe, kayak, fish, swim, snorkel, small boat

**RATING** Facilities ★★★★★ Location ★★★★★ Water activities ★★★★★

+00 353 (0) 9185256

www.wexfordswimmingpool.ie/caravan-park/

BEST IN
County
Wexford

# Eagle Point Camping ⑥
## Ballylickey, Bantry, West Cork

**Here's a setting that could have been plucked from the foothills of Lake Garda. Eagle Point's terraced grass pitches overlook the waters of the bay, with access to the Atlantic wilderness and some of the most spectacular green and rugged scenery in south-west Ireland.**

Bantry Bay is sheltered by peninsulas on either side. A boat launch makes the area easier to navigate by sailing dinghy, canoe or kayak. Several rivers, which feed into the bay, should be explored. Mackerel fishing from the rocks is popular. Campers caught most fish either side of high tide, although we preferred to fish from the canoe. Swimming is relatively safe along the shoreline. Activity centres are ideal for those that don't bring their own equipment, but it's a shame to come all this way without at least bringing a snorkel and mask, or a telescopic fishing rod. Whale-watching trips are available nearby, with boats leaving from Reen Pier, at the most southerly point of the west shore.

More than 100 pitches are spread about the eight-acre park. Facilities include a laundry room, dishwashing area, showers and toilets, TV room, playground, tennis court and football pitch. Bikes, scooters, skates and jet-skis aren't allowed on the site. A supermarket and garage are right outside the campsite. The ferry port at Cork is about 60 miles away.

*BEST IN County Cork*

## site info

**OPEN** April to October

**DIRECTIONS** Off the N71, 4 miles from Bantry just past Ballylickey, opposite Cronin's supermarket.

**YEP** Showers, toilets, tents, caravans, motorhomes, electric, shop (outside entrance), play area

**NO** Dogs, bar, restaurant

**ACTIVITIES** Canoe, kayak, fish, swim, snorkel, sailing dinghy

**RATING** Facilities ★★★★★ Location ★★★★★ Water activities ★★★★★

+00 353 (0) 2750630

www.eaglepointcamping.ie

# Berehaven Camper & Amenity Park ⑦
## Filane, Castletownbere, County Cork

**A golf course by the ocean, with its own campsite, boat launch and fabulous sea fishing. This private club is owned by several hundred members who make a small income from having converted part of their course into a campsite. If only more golf clubs had such insight. Castletownbere is at the entrance of Bantry Bay, a deep-water harbour. Although this region can suffer from the weather, these parts are sheltered by Bere Island and Hungry Hill, a section of the mountain range that runs down the centre of the peninsula.**

The clear waters are exceptional for diving and snorkelling, and the Atlantic is warmed by the Gulf Stream. By early autumn, water temperatures reach as high as 17°C, although it's still worth packing a wetsuit. Fishing is best from a canoe or kayak. Mackerel are most common, although these waters are rich with bass and cod. Boat-fishing day trips can be organised in the town. Small dinghies can launch from the campsite, but access for larger vessels is not great. Bear Island – a mile off shore – is the closest of several islands within about 12 miles that can be accessed by boat or canoe.

Golf-club members said they have plans to upgrade the camping area, although at the time of writing it has a rustic, clean charm and I couldn't see what upgrades were needed, other than more electric points. Showers and loos are inside the clubhouse. The nearest shop is two miles away. Dogs are allowed but must be kept on a lead. The family-run bar and restaurant overlook the bay and serve up food that's as good as the hospitality. Campers get reduced golf fees on the unique course, which requires players to hit across the watery bays. Members have excellent knowledge and enjoy passing on information about the surrounding area. Bere Island is just a few minutes away by ferry.

## site info

**OPEN** All year

**DIRECTIONS** On the R572, one mile before Castletownbere if arriving from the east. Signposted on the left.

**YEP** Dogs, showers, toilets, tents, caravans, motorhomes, electric, shop, bar, restaurant, equipment hire

**NO** Play area

**ACTIVITIES** Canoe, kayak, fish, swim, snorkel, sailing dinghy

**RATING** Facilities ★★★★★ Location ★★★★★ Water activities ★★★★★

+00 353 (0) 27 71957

www.berehavengolf.com

# Mannix Point Camping & Caravan Park 8
## Cahirciveen, Ring of Kerry

**Ireland's camp supreme. Rarely have I come across a site that receives so much affection from those that visit. Muircheartach Seosamh Breandan O'Muircheartaigh – otherwise known as Mortimer – set up the campsite in 1984 on a 'rough, wet, unproductive' piece of land, a short stroll from where he was born. He says he had almost no money, but buckets of enthusiasm. More than three decades on, he is owner of what many believe is the best campsite in Ireland. Situated on the western edge of the Iveragh Peninsula, in southwest Ireland, Mannix Point has 500 metres of waterfront.**

Aside from Mortimer, what makes Mannix special is the setting – it is by the sheltered Valentia Harbour, a natural body of water protected on all sides by either mountains or islands. The islands of Valentia and Beginis lie to the south-west like giant hands that have risen from the sea to defend the mainland from rogue Atlantic surges. Within 10 miles are almost 100 miles of jagged coastline (the apparent contradiction in distance is because the coastline wraps back towards itself again and again). Beaches and estuaries are surrounded by mountains, rivers, lakes and clean air.

And there's so much to do. Boating is the most fun. The Atlantic Sailing Club has made its home here. Campers can visit the club as long as they come with lifejackets and wetsuits and plenty arrive equipped with their own small sailing dinghies, sails, oars and kayaks. Fishing is excellent. Valentia waters hold the Irish records for conger eel and red sea bream. Whale-watching trips are available nearby.

Mannix Point complements everything else that is around. Other than the view, the highlight has to be the campers' sitting room, warmed in the evenings by turf fire and the gentle shrill of community. Guitars, a concertina, tin whistles, a keyboard and organs supplied by Mortimer help impromptu music sessions along. The laundry has two commercial washing machines and driers, and a sink for hand washing. The kitchen includes crockery, pottery, cookers, microwave, fridges and freezer. Tents, motorhomes and caravans are all provided with electricity, water and hard-standing pitches. The town of Cahirciveen is a 15-minute walk away. In Mortimer's own words, beware: one holiday here can result in a lifetime of return visits.

BEST IN
County Kerr

## site info

**OPEN** March to October

**DIRECTIONS** From Killarney on the N70 Ring-of-Kerry Road pass through the town of Cahirciveen and turn right at the campsite sign just before the Met Station.

**YEP** Dogs, showers, toilets, tents, caravans, motorhomes, electric

**NO** Shop, bar, restaurant, play area, equipment hire

**ACTIVITIES** Canoe, kayak, fish, swim, snorkel, sailing dinghy, surf

**RATING** Facilities ★★★★★ Location ★★★★★ Water activities ★★★★★

+00 353 (0) 66 9472806

www.campinginkerry.com

# scotland

I love Scotland. It begins at the border – a wild frontier, where nature takes care of itself. Few rules apply. Experienced campers overnight for free in the only UK region where wild camping remains legal. Rivers, canals and ditches offer unlimited public access for canoes and kayaks. Unlike England, Ireland and Wales, landowners cannot order boat users to leave their property.

Entry to this real life adventure-park is, of course, free, but seasoned campers come equipped. Scotland's national emblem, the thistle, epitomises a thorny, unyielding beauty. Two things undermine an appreciation of this wilderness – cold, wet summers and biting insects. Culicoides impunctatus, or 'midgies' as they are known locally, swarm upon high-season like a summer curse. Similar to the mosquito, these tiny, biting creatures aren't all bad. For starters, they don't transmit disease. More importantly, they're the main reason millions more tourists don't come to gorge themselves on the stunning landscapes. Fewer people camp in Scotland than anywhere else in the UK.

So how to avoid the midgies? Well, it's relatively simple really. Camp in a place where there aren't any. Look for areas with wind speeds of over six miles per hour and humidity below 60–75 per cent. For low humidity, visit in winter, spring or autumn. To find a breeze, pitch anywhere on the thousands of miles of Scottish coastline that are exposed to the elements. Some campsite owners advertise they are midgie-free in high season. But with several-thousand windswept islands to choose from, don't just follow the herd. If you're prepared to camp wild, you can afford to be fussy.

Most of the isles are uninhabited. They are dominated by turquoise blue sea, white sandy beaches and tranquil isolation, with only nature as a neighbour. These Caribbean-like treasures are truly unique. On the longest day of the year, the northern isles have no darkness. Orkney, with its archipelago of more than 70 islands, is a haven for angling. Swimming, diving and snorkelling should be compulsory in this region and the Outer Hebrides, looking out across the Atlantic Ocean, draw surfers from all over the world. The beaches and cliffs of Cape Wrath, Scotland's most north-westerly point, are a perfect midge-free zone. Battered by fresh winds, sea spray and rain, the Cape typifies the need to prepare for 'weather'. This is not the place for a comfort holiday and the thing to fear is forgetting to pack your wet gear (turn to page 11 for more on clothing).

For families craving adventure, Scotland is unbeatable value, offering pitches for as little as £8 per night at some of the hundreds of camps spread about lochs and rivers. Seasoned travellers venture inland during spring and autumn. Off-peak is bug free, and April and May can be as sunny as August. The scenery is as good as anything along the coast. Highland mountains and forests tower above cool, shimmering lochs where trout fishing, sailing, walking, cycling and canoeing help pass the time. For the more adventurous, there is white-water rafting, snowboarding, mountaineering and bungee jumping. Scotland is dominated by a fierce beauty thats just waiting to be discovered.

# Traigh Na Beirigh ①
Uig, Isle of Lewis, Hebrides HS2 9HS

**My favourite campsite in Scotland. No pictures or words can do it justice. Just promise to see it for yourself before you die. Kneep Bay is bordered by couch grass, wildflowers and dunes, with a sprinkling of sheep, golden eagles and Hebridean magic. The campsite is run by the Kneep Grazing Trust. There aren't too many rules (although generators are banned) so it's a good chance to see how people can be civilised when left to their own devices.**

The only thing that will keep you awake here (apart from wind on a bad-weather day) is the sweet sound of bad singing and campers playing mandolins, accordions and guitars round a campfire (bring your own firewood) or inside an awning. Surrounding islands can be explored from the shore by boat or canoe. There are many deserted beaches to discover, hidden from mainland view. The warm waters are relatively shallow at low tide. It's worth wearing a full wetsuit as the wind-chill can quickly cool damp skin on a cloudy day. Large seals and cormorants feed offshore at high tide. Handline or rod fishing is good at the site, but it's best on the neighbouring bay to the left of the campsite, as you look out to sea. A fish farm there seems to attract shoals of mackerel. It's a lovely walk along the shoreline, particularly with dogs. Surfing is not great, but there are some decent waves half a mile away.

New arrivals pitch anywhere, but not within six metres of another unit. With a little luck you can find a spot right on the beach edge. An elderly woman collects the money each night, as she has done for the last 20 years. Several campers complained about the lack of facilities, claiming they were paying a lot of money for 'a view'. Be warned: this is about as isolated and exposed a site as we've found. Although it's just 32 miles from Stornoway, it feels like the pit of beyond when the rain clouds and gales roll in. Seasonal campers bolt their caravans down on all four corners with 50-millimetre rope and wooden batons. If you're in a tent, come with plenty of pegs and try to make friends, so that you have someone to call on for shelter when you get blown away. There are two electrical points in the washroom where batteries and phones can be charged. Hot showers are available for a small fee. Wastewater points and plenty of fresh water are available. A community shop four miles away has everything you need, including a book-swap corner. Cycling over the mountains is wonderful, past a seawater loch and river.

# site info

**OPEN** April to October

**DIRECTIONS** 3-hour ferry from mainland Scotland (Ullapool) to Isle of Lewis (Stornaway). Once on Lewis, leave the B8011 and follow signs for Kneep.

**YEP** Dogs, showers, toilets, tents, caravans, motorhomes

**NO** Electric, shop, bar, restaurant, play area, equipment hire

**ACTIVITIES** Canoe, kayak, fish, swim, snorkel, sailing dinghy, surf (poor)

**RATING** Facilities ★★★★★ Location ★★★★★ Water activities ★★★★★

01851 672265

No website

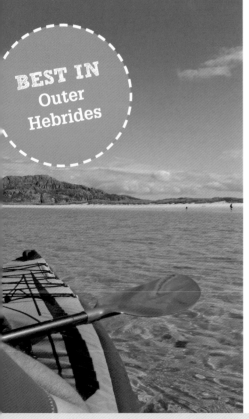

BEST IN
Outer
Hebrides

# Horgabost Camping  ②

Horgabost, Isle of Harris, Hebrides, HS3 3HR

In 2011, Ben Fogle tried – and failed – to buy the uninhabited Outer Hebridean island where he lived for a year for the BBC reality show *Castaway*. Taransay was sold for £2 million within two weeks of going on the market. The dunes at Horgabost Camping, on the Isle of Harris, look out onto the beach where Fogle stayed, separated by just two miles of clear, blue sea, easily navigable by kayak or boat on a calm day. The two islands make remarkable neighbours. Harris, world famous for its tweed; Taransay, for 15 minutes of TV fame. Horgabost is the chance to savour both.

White beaches stretch for miles in all directions. Walk across the headland to the east of the campsite for a closer view of Taransay. Kayaking is the best way to see the coast and its surrounding islands. Trail spinners around the rocks to catch pollack and mackerel. Further out you can expect to hook cod, whiting and even ling. Harris Sea Angling provides trips and advice. Waves for surfing and windsurfing are best at low tide.

Campers find their own pitches and pay at the front gate via an honesty box. Tents get the prime spots on the front dunes, running the gauntlet of violent squalls that can rip up pegs and canvas. Crofters deliver seafood suppers to order, as no shops are nearby. There is no wastewater dump, but the port a few miles away will accommodate. No electrical hook-up for caravans and motorhomes, but there are four electric points in the washroom area for charging batteries and phones. Fogle described weather that altered the landscape 'like an artist's canvas … talc-white sandy beaches and the turquoise waters more striking than any Caribbean or Pacific island'. Horgabost has all of that – but for a tad less than £2 million.

## site info

**OPEN** All year

**DIRECTIONS** On the A859 between Seilebost and Buirgh (catch a car ferry from Ullapool).

**YEP** Dogs, showers, toilets, tents, caravans, motorhomes

**NO** Electric, shop, bar, restaurant, play area, equipment hire

**ACTIVITIES** Canoe, surf, kayak, fish, swim, snorkel, dinghy

**RATING** Facilities ★★★★★ Location ★★★★★ Water activities ★★★★★

No phone – just turn up

No website

# Dunnet Bay Caravan Club  ③
## Dunnet, Thurso, Highlands, KW14 8XD

**The most northerly point in mainland Britain becomes wilder than a swarm of wasps in a jam jar when squalls move over the bay. But if you arrive here on a beautiful day, it's possible to believe that the sun might shine forever. Dunes, white-tipped surf and fresh air are a fine combination for campers who come equipped to weather it out. Walking along the beach on the summer nights when it never really gets dark – known locally as the 'simmer dim' – is a treat.**

Anglers have a choice of fishing by boat or from the beach. Fishing at the campsite is best for flounders, bass and sea trout. Mussels and lugworm make bait and can be found at low tide. Rocky headlands around the bay are good for casting. Kayaking, canoeing and surfing are all good, especially for beginners as there aren't too many hazards. Dunnet Head is a popular location for coasteering (see page 32), as the rocks and cliffs provide fine conditions for this swimming, climbing and trekking combo.

Fifty-seven pitches are serviced by showers, toilets and a laundry. As with all Caravan Club sites, the place is spotlessly clean. Non-members are accepted. Although the area is secluded, the village of Dunnet is only a mile away on the A836. The same road leads towards John O'Groats in the east and Thurso in the west. The cliff top at Dunnet Head, a few miles away, has views across the water to Scapa Flow in the Orkneys. On a clear day, you can almost see along the entire width of this northern cap to Cape Wrath on the west point. Day trips from John O'Groats or Scrabster to the Orkneys (an archipelago of 70 islands) are easy by boat. The nearest shops are in Castletown village, three miles towards Thurso. There are supermarkets in Thurso and Wick.

## site info

**OPEN** April to October

**DIRECTIONS** From the east (John O'Groats) on A836 – site on right, half a mile past Dunnet Village. From the west (Thurso) on A836 – site on left about 2.5 miles past Castletown village.

**YEP** Dogs, electric, showers, toilets, tents, caravans, motorhomes

**NO** Bar, restaurant, play area, equipment hire

**ACTIVITIES** Canoe, kayak, fish, swim, snorkel, surf

**RATING** Facilities ★★★★★ Location ★★★★★ Water activities ★★★★★

01847 821319

www.caravanclub.co.uk
Search 'Dunnet Bay'

# Broomfield Holiday Park  ❹

## West Lane, Ullapool, Highlands IV26 2SX

**Broomfield Holiday Park rests on Loch Broom like an ornate transit camp en route to paradise (Uig, Lewis, see page 64). If I had six months to live, I'd spend it in this port town, soaking up the fishing, pubs and cafés on Shore Street, waiting for the clouds to break over the Outer Hebrides. Ullapool is on the north-west coast of the Highlands, close to where the sun sets over the Summer Isles. Roads out of Ullapool track south to Skye and Gairloch, or north towards Cape Wrath. The Ullapool Ferry cruises west for the Isle of Lewis – the most beautiful island in Britain.**

This is a place to anticipate travel, rather than to arrive. Boats, seals and seabirds are permanently drifting past on the horizon. The campsite beach is easy for putting in sea-kayaks, particularly at high tide. For larger craft there's a launch a few hundred metres away. Fishing is excellent either from the shore or boat. Salmon, trout, pollack, haddock, mackerel and skate can be caught. Tackle shops have plenty of good information on seasonal bait and boat trips.

Most of the 140 pitches look out onto the loch. Hook-ups are available across more than 12 acres of level grass. Demand for space on the waterfront is high, so there's plenty of room at the back. Some campers complain pitch fees are too expensive, but few sites have quite so much going for them. The ground beneath the grass is rocky, so use 15-centimetre nails, rather than weak tent pegs. Shower and toilet blocks are clean. The town's shops, cafes and restaurants are within a few minutes' walk away. The ferry to Stornoway, on the Isle of Lewis, leaves three times a day in the summer. I keep an eye on the weather forecast. If clear skies are predicted, then Lewis is well worth a day trip. When fine weather sets in for a week, it's time to pick up, pack up, and buy an open return for the white sands of Uig. Divine.

## site info

**OPEN** March to September

**DIRECTIONS** Follow the A835 into Ullapool. Drive past the port on Shore Street to the end of the town.

**YEP** Dogs, electric, showers, toilets, tents, caravans, motorhomes, play area

**NO** Bar, restaurant, equipment hire

**ACTIVITIES** Canoe, kayak, fish, swim, snorkel, sailing dinghy

**RATING** Facilities ★★★★★ Location ★★★★★ Water activities ★★★★★

01854 612020

www.broomfieldhp.com

# Sands Caravan & Camping  ⑤
## Gairloch, Highlands IV21 2DL

**You must be decisive here. You have fifty acres of land from which to choose your pitch, among towering dunes of sand and grass. We drove around, settled and moved; and then moved again. The highest pitches have the best views over the Torridon Mountain and across towards Lewis and Skye. The vast campsite sits on the edge of the Atlantic Ocean and Loch Gairloch. Gairloch translates from the Gaelic as 'short loch'. Its six-mile length can be navigated by boat past the villages of Gairloch, Charlestown, Kerrysdale, Shieldaig, Badachro and Port Henderson.**

A large on-site jetty provides a launch for yachts, and is a good base for sea fishing. Staff are knowledgeable on tides, winds and safe launching. Gairloch Boat Club, a few miles away, also offers helpful advice. Sands River on the site's western boundary is ideal for anglers, especially beginners or young ones. The river has eels and small trout that can be fished out with worms. Sands Loch spans 2 acres, and can be fished free of charge by campers, without a permit. Rods, tackle and local angling guides are available in the camp shop. Most loch and river fishing in the area is governed by the Gairloch Angling Club. Permits are available from Gairloch Harbour. Kayak fishing is popular all around this part of the coastline. Boats and paddles can be hired from the site shop. Sea-fishing trips, whale-spotting expeditions and trips to the puffin colonies are available nearby.

There are 250 pitches. For bad weather, the lower camping areas offer the best shelter. In fine weather they provide easy access to the water and surf. Excellent facilities include large, clean toilet and shower blocks, a laundry with washing machines, covered indoor cooking and eating area, a games and TV room and bikes for hire. The licensed shop (April to September) sells everything from fresh bread and Calor gas to wetsuits and books. Miles of sandy beach, rockpools and an on-site playground means there's loads for kids to do. Campsite management organise fun events, such as sandcastle competitions, throughout the summer. Staff are very professional and friendly. Ullapool is just over an hour's drive away, with regular ferries to the Hebridean islands.

## site info

**OPEN** April to October

**DIRECTIONS** Leave the A832 for the B8021 at the Gairloch Heritage Museum and follow signs for camping.

**YEP** Dogs, showers, toilets, tents, caravans, motorhomes, electric, shop, play area, equipment hire

**NO** Bar, restaurant

**ACTIVITIES** Canoe, kayak, fish, swim, snorkel, sailing dinghy

**RATING** Facilities ★★★★★ Location ★★★★★ Water activities ★★★★★

01445 712152

www.sandscaravanandcamping.co.uk

# Skye Camping & Caravanning Club Site
## Arnisort, Edinbane, Portree, Isle of Skye IV51 9PS

**The largest of the Inner Hebridean islands rises from the Atlantic like a barnacled shipwreck in a storm. Ocean waves smash against stone peninsulas, seemingly battering their way towards Skye's rocky peaks. Cuillin Hills dominate the centre and attract climbers, walkers and cyclists of all ages and abilities. The campsite is on a working croft in the north, overlooking Loch Greshornish.**

Early morning walks along the loch and meadows are wonderful. The site is on the eastern side of the sea loch. Fishing, sailing, kayaking and swimming are all possible directly from the park. The mouth of the loch, where it meets the Atlantic, is about three miles away by canoe or sailing boat. Fishing is free. Most people use spinners or lures to catch mackerel, pollock and the occasional salmon and sea trout.

They call this 'the friendly club' and there's no disputing the helpfulness of the wardens, although they can be a tad overbearing if you park your unit a few inches off-centre or leave an engine running for more than 30 seconds. Choose from hard-standing and grass areas. Tents and small campervans in the lower field get the best loch views, just in front of two wooden cabin pods. Facilities are incredibly clean. A huge shower and toilet block at the centre of the campsite means no one has to walk too far. A snack van turns up a couple of times a week with cod and chips. A mile down the road is a pub, better value and a nice retreat at the end of the day when Skye's weather turns black. The camp shop sells plenty of basics, including chicken and duck eggs laid on-site.

*BEST IN*
*Inner*
*Hebrides*

## site info

**OPEN** April to October

**DIRECTIONS** Off the A850, between Bernisdale and Arnisort.

**YEP** Dogs, showers, toilets, tents, caravans, motorhomes, electric, shop

**NO** Bar, restaurant, play area, equipment hire

**ACTIVITIES** Canoe, kayak, fish, swim, snorkel, sail

**RATING** Facilities ★★★☆☆ Location ★★★★★ Water activities ★★★★☆

01470 582230

www.campingandcaravanningclub. co.uk/skye

# Sligachan Campsite
## Sligachan Carbost, Isle of Skye IV47 8SW

**This is a campsite for hardy souls, but it offers one of the best views in Britain. The river winds its way from the base of the campsite out towards the Cuillin Mountains that tower over Loch Sligachan. It's a dramatic scene that entices most campers to take a hike. The hotel has been accommodating mountaineers and walkers for almost 200 years.**

The Sligachan River is fast-flowing and rocky, but generally too shallow for canoes or kayaks. Fishing is OK in the loch, although the river is generally unproductive unless there's been heavy rainfall and a high tide. Salmon, sea-trout and brown-trout fishing are most common. Information on permits is available from the hotel. We met campers with rods, but no one that had fished with any success.

The campsite, like the mountain range, is exposed, but facilities are good. Toilets, showers, washing machine and tumble dryer are all clean. Hook-ups are available to at least 15 pitches on hard-standing. The warden is always helpful. Shops at Portree are almost 10 miles away, so try to arrive well stocked up. For food and drink, the hotel and Seamus Bar are close, on the other side of the A87 road. There is a climbing and mountaineering museum in the hotel. The bar famously stocks several hundred malt whiskies, and there's a play-park and indoor games for the kids for those cold evenings. Sligachan's popularity among climbers dates back to the late-1800s, as these relatively modest-looking peaks are reputedly as tough to take on as the Alps. Novice climbers are encouraged not to bother. An annual running race is held in July from the hotel to the nearest hill, Glamaig, and back again.

## site info

**OPEN** April to October

**DIRECTIONS** Cross the Skye Bridge and continue to follow the A87 to Sligachan.

**YEP** Dogs, showers, toilets, tents, caravans, motorhomes, restaurant, play area, bar, electric

**NO** Shop, equipment hire

**ACTIVITIES** Fish

**RATING** Facilities ★★★★★ Location ★★★★★ Water activities ★★★★★

01478 650204

www.sligachan.co.uk/sligachan-campsite.php

# The Croft Caravan & Campsite 8
## 4 Back of Keppoch, Arisaig, Highlands PH39 4NS

**A unique gathering occurs each summer at this shallow cove off Scotland's west coast. Pods of pilot whales swim off the bay during August and September. The campsite is a working farm, run by a husband-and-wife team. They've been welcoming back regulars for more than 30 years. Livestock roam the peaty grass meadows, which lead down to the white-sand beach. The Gulf Stream warms the sea and air, making it a great place for watersports.**

Mackerel and cod are easily caught on a handline from a boat at high tide about 500 metres offshore. Surrounding rocks are best for rod fishing. Kids love fishing the rock pools for tiddlers. Canoes and kayaks can be left on the beach within easy view, although the tide can come in very fast if you're not watching.

Things get busy in August, but there are four neighbouring beach camps within three miles, which are almost just as good. The toilet block is small but clean, and there are no showers. The owners will provide a free cable extension if, like mine, yours comes up short. All pitches are grass, with views across the islands of Skye, Egg and Rum. Calmac Ferries offer an excellent service to 22 islands just off the west coast, which makes this an ideal base for summer island hopping.

**BEST IN Highlands**

## site info

**OPEN** April to October

**DIRECTIONS** Leave the A830 onto the B8008. Turn into a country lane at signpost for Back of Keppoch by bus shelter. Site is 500 metres on right.

**YEP** Dogs, electric, toilets, tents, caravans, motorhomes

**NO** Showers, shop, bar, restaurant, play area, equipment hire

**ACTIVITIES** Canoe, kayak, fish, swim, snorkel, sailing dinghy

**RATING** Facilities ★★☆☆☆ Location ★★★★★ Water activities ★★★★★

01687 450200

No website

# Linnhe Lochside Holidays ⑨
Corpach, Fort William, Highlands PH33 7NL

'Fort William is the outdoor capital of the UK,' they told us when we arrived at Linnhe reception. High-octane fun doesn't come wrapped in modesty in the Highlands: Ben Nevis, skiing, championship mountain bike tracks, river rafting, fishing, trekking and sailing. Ranked by the AA as the best campsite in Scotland, this is a base for adventure. Don't doubt the credentials – the Loch Eil canyon is where scenes for *Braveheart* and *Harry Potter* were shot.

Otters, deer and birds of prey appear like ghosts at dawn within view of the camp. A slipway for boats leads onto the private shore of Loch Eil. Tidal waters feed into Loch Linnhe, via a right-angled bend at Fort William, and then ebb out into the Atlantic, passed Oban, about 30 miles away. Rods and tackle are available for hire or sale from the camp shop. Angling is free. Pike fishing is a favourite, although much patience is needed. If you like to catch dinner before dark, mackerel feed off the pier next to the Caledonian Canal, a five-minute drive away. Locals cast spinners an hour before high tide, close to where the canal meets the loch. Kayaking and canoeing are good from the campsite.

The level, hard-standing pitches are spread across terraced gardens, lined by conifers, firs and flowers. The loch is visible from all angles. Pitches T1–5 are best for those in motorised units. Tents get closest to the water on the grass. Toilets, showers and laundry are very clean. Cubicles with baths are available for a small fee, as a treat for those weary after the day's adventures. The licensed shop stocks most basics and freshly baked bread is on order daily.

## site info

**OPEN** December to October

**DIRECTIONS** Off the A830, between Kinlocheil and Corpach.

**YEP** Dogs, showers, toilets, tents, caravans, motorhomes, electric, shop, play area

**NO** Bar, restaurant, equipment hire

**LAUNCH** Canoe, kayak, fish, swim, snorkel, sailing dinghy, yacht

**ACTIVITIES** Facilities ★★★★★
Location ★★★★★ Water activities
★★★★★

01397 772376

www.linnhe-lochside-holidays.co.uk

# Loch Ness Holiday Park  10
## Easter Port Clair, Invermoriston, Highlands IV63 7YE

**If Nessie floats your boat, come with an open mind and a good imagination; the ripples and sunlight will do the rest. There's more fresh water here than in all the lakes of England and Wales combined. The lake's deeper than the height of London's BT Tower, too. Nowhere is quite like Loch Ness for contemplation and daydreaming.**

Loch Ness trout and salmon can be tough to hook, so take time with knots when tackling up. Landing nets and rods are available for hire. Safe wooden jetties, as well as a ramp opposite reception, make launching canoes, yachts and powered craft easy. Melbourne, in Australia, is famous for four seasons in a day – they pass here in an hour. Cruisers and yachts sail silently from dawn to dusk, apparently oblivious to the weather and big skies. Pragmatic campers, who don't care for Highland myths and monsters, come to weather watch. Don't knock it – Scotch mist rolls in on a sunny, day, it crawls over the mountains, down to the loch surface and then up and away as fast as it arrived, like a deathly scene from *Lord of the Rings*.

The park is the only campsite on the loch, and it traces the shoreline between the trees like a voyeur's hideaway. Two rows of pitches are located either side of the site's narrow access road. Waterside is the prime location, especially if you want to fish, although the pitches further back are almost as good, with great views. Take care when going down from camp to the tiny pebble beaches, as the rocks can get slippery when wet. Loch-side wood cabins (fittingly named after characters from *Lord of the Rings*) can sleep a family of four, but tents aren't catered for. The showers get my vote for the best in Scotland: spotlessly clean and warm. Each cubicle has a carpeted entrance. The kids' playground is a decent size. Tasty meals are served into the evening in the restaurant-bar. Monster good.

# site info

**OPEN** All year (subject to weather)

**DIRECTIONS** Signposted off the A82 between Fort Augustus and Invermoriston.

**YEP** Dogs, showers, toilets, caravans, motorhomes, electric, shop, bar, restaurant, play area, rod hire

**NO** Tents

**ACTIVITIES** Canoe, kayak, fish, swim, snorkel, sailing dinghy

**RATING** Facilities ★★★★★ Location ★★★★★ Water activities ★★★★★

01320 351207

www.lochnessholidaypark.co.uk

# Banff Links Caravan Park
Banff, Aberdeenshire AB45 2JJ

**Surfers unite! This is a beach campsite with a reputation for cleanliness and big waves. Aberdeenshire Council takes great pride in ensuring fans of watersports enjoy their stay at Inverboyndie Beach, on the north-east coast of Aberdeenshire. The town of Banff, which claims to be one of the sunniest and driest in Scotland, is just over a mile east of the campsite. Macduff village is a little further west, with its beautiful arch bridge spanning the River Deveron.**

Experienced surfers arrive on this exposed north-facing strip from all over Scotland. Surfing from the campsite is possible at any time of day. Waves are best between low to mid tide. Caution is needed around the rocks. The water can be incredibly cold on this coast, even in summer, so good wetsuits are essential. Moray Firth is an outstanding place for fishing in Scotland. River Deveron enters the firth between Banff and Macduff and is one of the best salmon rivers in Scotland. Its lower reaches can be navigated from the campsite, but it's wise to set off early. Banff-based Deveron Canoe Club runs paddling outings for both kayaks and open canoes along the coast and upstream, and offers advice.

More than 80 pitches open from April to October, most of them with electric. Tents, caravans and motorhomes are accepted. Showers, toilets, laundry and washing-up facilities are OK. Dogs are allowed. Boat trips and boat hire are available from Macduff to see dolphins and whales along the Moray coast. The coastal paths run alongside the campsite. The council recently gave up managing the campsite, but there do not appear to be plans to close it. Cycling and walking are good.

## site info

**OPEN** April to October

**DIRECTIONS** Turn off the A98 west of Banff and head towards Inverboyndie Beach. Campsite is on the western shore.

**YEP** Dogs, electric, showers, toilets, tents, caravans, motorhomes

**NO** Shop, bar, restaurant, play area, equipment hire

**ACTIVITIES** Canoe, surf, kayak, fish, swim, sailing dinghy

**RATING** Facilities ★★★★★ Location ★★★★★ Water activities ★★★★★

01261 812228

www.aberdeenshire.gov.uk/ caravanparks/locations/Banff.asp

BEST IN Aberdeenshire

# Fraserburgh Esplanade Caravan Park
## The Esplanade, Fraserburgh, Aberdeenshire AB43 5EU

**Sea air, fishing and surfing are the big three for health-seeking campers at Fraserburgh. Europe's largest shellfish port made its home on one of the best surfing beaches in Scotland. The site is in north-east corner of Aberdeenshire, 40 miles north of Aberdeen and 17 miles from Peterhead. Despite being rather close to the Young's seafood factory, the campsite looks out across a fabulous sandy beach.**

East-facing shores provide consistent surf all year round. Spring and winter see the best of the waves. Autumn tides are kinder for rookies when the water is warmer and waves are smaller. The prevailing offshore wind is from the south. Kite surfing has taken off in Fraserburgh, with the town hosting several international events. Fishing is possible all around the campsite. The harbour can be productive, although it's easy to lose line and gear on the bottom. Cod will bite along the beach at night with lug. Kayaks and canoes are launched from the shore next to the campsite, and provide the best angling. Swimming from the beach is relatively safe, but care needs to be taken.

About 50 pitches cater for vans and tents, with and without electrical hook-up. Showers and toilets are in good condition, and have baby-changing facilities. Free racquets and tennis balls are provided to caravan park customers for the courts opposite the park. This may not continue for much longer, as the council has recently relinquished control of the park. The large football park opposite the caravan park will remain available.

## site info

**OPEN** April to October

**DIRECTIONS** Head towards Fraserburgh Beach, either via the A98 or A90. Find the campsite in the north-west corner of the beach.

**YEP** Dogs, showers, toilets, tents, caravans, motorhomes, electric

**NO** Shop, bar, restaurant, play area

**ACTIVITIES** Canoe, surf, kayak, fish, swim, sailing dinghy

**RATING** Facilities ★★★★★ Location ★★★★★ Water activities ★★★★★

01346 510041

www.aberdeenshire.gov.uk/
caravanparks/locations/fraserburgh.asp

# Cobleland Camping and Caravanning Site (13)
Station Road, Gartmore, Stirlingshire FK8 3UX

**Salmon fishing is one of Scotland's favourite pastimes and this is a unique setting for having a go. Cobleland Camping is within the Queen Elizabeth Forest Park, in the Loch Lomond and Trossachs National Park.**

Angling within the park boundary is free. The River Forth was listed as one of the top salmon producers in Scotland in 2010. Fishing lasts from February to October and the Scottish brown trout season begins in March. Depending on rain and water levels, it's also possible to canoe or kayak on the river. It rises in Loch Ard and flows east for almost 30 miles, past the campsite and out into the Atlantic, between the Isle of May and Bass Rock, at Forth of Firth. From Stirling it becomes tidal. Kids enjoy swimming and paddling about on warm summer days.

More than 100 pitches are set among ancient oak trees. This is one of 20 forest sites run by the Camping and Caravanning Club on behalf of the Forestry Commission Estate. Toilets and showers are excellent. Facilities include a TV room, laundry, recreation hall and children's play area. Dogs are allowed. Aberfoyle village is nearby. Just north of the village is David Marshall Lodge where ospreys can be seen. Stirling is 20 minutes away and Glasgow 45 minutes. Come with good walking shoes and lots of energy. The expansive forest trails can get muddy when it rains.

## site info

**OPEN** April to October

**DIRECTIONS** Leave the A81 west, just north of Gartmore and south of the bridge over the River Forth. The campsite is about 300 metres away.

**YEP** Dogs, showers, toilets, tents, caravans, motorhomes, play area, electric, shop

**NO** Bar, restaurant

**ACTIVITIES** Canoe, kayak, fish, swim,

**RATING** Facilities ★★★★★ Location ★★★★★ Water activities ★★★★★

0845 130 8224

www.campingandcaravanningclub.co.uk
Search 'Cobleland Campsite'

BEST IN Stirlingshire

# Luss Camping & Caravanning Club Site  14
## Loch Lomond, Argyll, G83 8NT

**Loch Lomond is to Glasgow what Southend-on-Sea is to London's East End: a playground for the people of the city. All similarities end there. This gateway to the Highlands is inside 720 square miles controlled by Loch Lomond and the Trossachs National Park. The campsite is in the village of Luss, on the west shore of the loch, Britain's second largest freshwater lake (after Lough Neagh, in Northern Ireland) spanning 27 square miles of water.**

Thirty-odd islands can be reached by canoe, kayak or dingy, many from the campsite. The white pebble beach is shadowed by pines and craggy peaks. Water is at its warmest in September, when swimmers can ditch the wetsuit. The loch is clear enough to snorkel in. Fish tend to migrate to the southern shore, although catching them isn't easy. Anglers skilled in the art of trolling (dragging a lure or bait) behind a powered boat have most success on cloudy days.

Luss is a site for families, although some of the more secluded waterside areas have an arty feel about them, as if they were crafted by writers, poets or painters who crave only lapping water and their thoughts for company. The best pitches are among bushes, beside the stony beach. Quiet is disturbed now and again by the occasional seaplane. Flights are from a watersports centre a short drive from the camp. Campsite facilities are clean, including the large toilet and shower blocks. Younger kids have access to a play area.

BEST IN
Argyll

## site info

**OPEN** April to October

**DIRECTIONS** Signposted on the right off the A82 (travelling north from Glasgow).

**YEP** Dogs, showers, toilets, tents, caravans, motorhomes, electric, play area

**NO** Large shop, bar, restaurant, equipment hire

**ACTIVITIES** Canoe, kayak, fish, swim, snorkel, sailing dinghy

**RATING** Facilities ★★★★ Location ★★★★★ Water activities ★★★★

01436 860658

www.campingandcaravanningclub.co.uk/luss

# wales

**If I could, I'd crown Wales the official World Home of Camping. There are more campsites per square mile here than anywhere else in the UK. And what landscapes. Wales is like a giant kaleidoscope – only it's no illusion. Three national parks, verdant valleys, mountain peaks, miles of sand dunes, Celtic heritage and a mother tongue spoken by a quarter of the population, crammed into 8,000 square miles.**

My first trip here was as a kid on a family holiday. We arrived from Gloucestershire in a white Volkswagen Variant. It started raining at the border and rarely stopped. But I never got over the contrast between the Wye Valley, the torrents of white water at Swallow Falls, the dark peaks of the Black Mountains and beams of sunlight through moody clouds over Tenby Sands.

More than 100 rivers, 500 lakes and 746 miles of coastline surround the Snowdonia National Park in the north, and the Brecon Beacons National Park in the south. The River Usk winds its way through the latter to meet the spectacular River Severn. The Severn is the longest river in Britain (220 miles) and it is famous for the Severn Bore, an inland tidal wave. Camping along its grassy bank, you can almost touch the ancient past of flint tools, oracles and dangerous wild animals. Heading for the north coast, the 46-mile Llangollen Canal is much less intimidating, but it can get busy in the midsummer. Braving the crowds to see the Pontcysyllte Aqueduct is a must. The cast iron, man-made chute suspends the canal 40 metres above the ground on top of 19 arches that span the River Dee. At the very least, walk over it.

The Welsh coast is heavenly from top to bottom. Llandudno, Colwyn Bay, Prestatyn and Anglesey are furthest north. The southward beach trail leads from here down to my favourite Welsh region, Gwynedd. Apart from Mount Snowdon, Barmouth, and some of the finest salmon fishing in the UK, there's camping at Bala, on the largest inland lake in Wales. The coastal road continues its way down into Ceredigion and Cardigan Bay, and to the Pembrokeshire Coast National Park, which has more award-winning beaches than anywhere else in the UK. Swansea Bay, the Mumbles and the fabulous Gower Peninsula cap off the beach trail semi-circle.

Be sure to pack sturdy wind-breaks. The winds seem to blow more here than anywhere else I've visited and there is near constant rainfall in the highest reaches of Snowdonia. The temperature around the coast is average for the UK. February to September are the driest months. Coastal winds make surfing and sailing a fantastic way to spend the days. Opportunities for sea kayaking, canoeing, fishing and swimming are unlimited and at just an hour's drive from Manchester, two hours from London and 90 minutes (by ferry) from Dublin, access to this water world is easy.

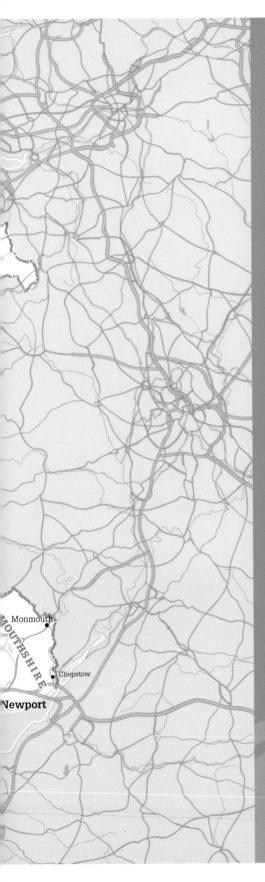

Monmouth

Chepstow

Newport

# Aberafon ①

Gyrn Goch, Caernarfon, Gwynedd, LL54 5PN

**Grassy meadows fall down to a private beach beneath the peak of Gyrn Goch on the Llyn peninsula. A fast-moving stream cuts through the 15-acre valley park, before flushing out into the sea beside the campsite.**

Everything is possible here – swimming, fishing, snorkelling, canoeing and surfing. A launch ramp accommodates larger boats. Rays can be caught when line-fishing from a sea kayak. The beach is good for bass and the rocky terrain is one of the few places in the UK where turbot can be caught from the beach (best during spring and mid-October). Bait up with frozen sand eel and mackerel. For larger fish, try a small whiting fillet. Use a lead weight across the surf, not too far from the shore, where the fish feed. Kids can have fun crabbing along the shore. Surfing is OK, mostly for short, fast rides. The surf from the right will provide a longer ride.

Choose from pitches next to the beach or up high overlooking Caernarfon Bay. Five acres are sheltered with level pitches. The facilities block has showers and shaving points. Laundry and dishwashing facilities are good and there is a small shop stocking the essentials, and a play area for kids. The only thing that keeps this place off the map is the narrow, winding drive to reach it. The largest vehicles struggle to navigate their way down here. Beach fires can be lit to keep warm on those cold evenings. Public footpaths lead up to the Yr Eifl mountains. The nearest pub and groceries are just over a mile way and there are supermarkets at Pwllheli. Snowdon is 20 minutes away.

## site info

**OPEN** April to October

**DIRECTIONS** Take the coast road 10 miles south of Caernarfon, to the village of Clynnog-Fawr. Carry on for 1 mile to the hamlet of Gyrn Goch. Passing through, you will see a farm on the right with a red corrugated shed, by the side of which is a gate. Go through the gate and follow the track.

**YEP** Dogs, showers, toilets, tents, caravans, motorhomes, electric, shop, play area

**NO** Restaurant, bar, equipment hire

**ACTIVITIES** Canoe, kayak, fish, swim, sailing dinghy, surf

**RATING** Facilities ★★★★★ Location ★★★★★ Water activities ★★★★★

01286 660295

www.aberafon.co.uk

# Abererch Sands ②
## Pwllheli, Gwynedd LL53 6PJ

**This place is rough and romantic. I've never seen so many cuddling couples along a single stretch of beach. The campsite is full of noise and surf. Abererch Sands is on the Lleyn Peninsula – four miles of coves and shoreline, spanning the north Wales coast across Cardigan Bay and Snowdonia.**

Other than for walking and sunbathing, people come to kayak, fish and water-ski. Some effort has been made to protect the sand dunes with weather-beaten fencing, which adds to the rustic charm. Fishing from the beach is best at dawn and dusk during the summer season. Bait up with squid and crab. Dogfish, flounder, dabs, thornback, mackerel and gurnard are common. Bass can be caught using lures. Try float fishing with small mackerel as bait for larger fish. The beach is relatively safe for swimming, as the area isn't renowned for currents, but take care. It's also a great place to fish from a sea kayak. The prevailing south-westerly wind blows cross-shore, which is ideal for windsurfing and sailing. Only small dinghies can be taken onto the beach. Yachting events are held, but there's no launch area from the campsite. Several clubs along the beach offer sailing advice. Waves are mostly poor for surfing. Unless you are a surfing rookie, try Porth Ceiriad or Porth Neigwl.

Almost 100 pitches have electrical hook-ups, some available for tents. A railway line passes close to the site, but the trains are relatively quiet. Facilities include an indoor swimming pool, gym, snooker room, a washing machine, a sink for washing dishes, a self-service shop and a children's playground. Pwllheli has shops, restaurants and pubs, and is only two miles down the road.

## site info

**OPEN** March to October

**DIRECTIONS** Turn off the A497 towards the coast at the roundabout, 2 miles east of Pwllheli.

**YEP** Dogs, showers, toilets, tents, caravans, motorhomes, equipment hire, electric, play area

**NO** Bar, restaurant

**ACTIVITIES** Canoe, kayak, fish, swim, sailing dinghy, surf

**RATING** Facilities ★★★★★ Location ★★★★★ Water activities ★★★★★

01758 612327

www.abererch-sands.co.uk

# Tyn Ddol Camping & Caravanning Club CS

## Llanystumdwy, Criccieth, Gwynedd LL52 0SP

**There's something wholly holy about the village of Llanystumdwy and the river that runs through it. The Tyn Ddol campsite sits next to the river, on the southern coast of the Llyn Peninsula. The river is 'Afon Dwyfor', which means 'big holy river', while Llanystumdwy translates as 'church at the bend in the river'.**

This is one of best sea trout rivers in Wales. Large fish can be caught with spinners, surface lures, floats or flies. Permits are available from local tackle shops. Night fly-fishing is worth a try. Worms work well from a float, cast along the bank to bob along with the current (float trotting) when the water is high. The salmon run starts in September. Depending on the water flow, experienced canoeists and kayakers either travel upstream to Cwm Pennant or come down in the opposite direction. Ask for advice before attempting this, as some sections are extremely dangerous, with Grade 3 and 4 rapids and weirs. Canoes can't get access to the sea from here.

The one-acre camping area caters for just five pitches. This is a certificated site for members of the Camping and Caravanning Club. A stone crossing leads across the river to a tea garden and café on the bank opposite, which makes for a relaxing afternoon. The Feathers Inn is a few minutes' walk away and serves great food and beer. Across the road from the pub is the Lloyd George Museum. Llanystumdwy is the home town of Lloyd George, who was Britain's Prime Minister from 1916–1922. The beaches at Criccieth are two miles away, and Black Rock Sands is four miles further on (see page 92). The river leaves the village via and under the A497, where it joins the River Dwyfach to become the Dwyfor Estuary, about a mile from the campsite. Llyn Coastal Path passes through the village too, and it's possible to walk some of the way along the riverbank.

## site info

**OPEN** March to October

**DIRECTIONS** Take A497 from Criccieth towards Pwllheli. Turn into Llanystumdwy village and follow the road over the bridge. The site is after the bend on the left-hand side of the road.

**YEP** Dogs, showers, toilets, tents, caravans, motorhomes

**NO** Electric, shop, bar, restaurant, play area, equipment hire

**ACTIVITIES** Canoe, kayak, fish

**RATING** Facilities ★★☆☆☆
Location ★★★☆☆ Water activities ★★★☆☆

01766 523092

www.campingandcaravanningclub.co.uk
Search 'Tyn Ddol'

RIVER
ALL CHILDREN
MUST BE SUPERVISED
AT ALL TIMES

# Black Rock Sands Touring & Camping Park

## Morfa Bychan, Porthmadog, Gwynedd LL49 9YH

**The dunes of Black Rock Sands shield the campsite from the waves that break along this two-mile white-sand beach. Nearby Criccieth and the port town of Porthmadog are a few miles away in either direction along Cardigan Bay.**

Camping is on the western end of the beach, next to the rocks. On a calm day, it's possible to canoe or kayak east along the beach towards the Glaslyn Estuary. Porthmadog port, built on reclaimed land, is a two-mile paddle from the beach along the River Glaslyn. Currents around the estuary can be dangerous. The waves are often big enough to surf, but this is not an area renowned for great boarding. The park is ideal for overnight stays with boats and jet skis, which only incur a small extra charge. All watercraft and powerboats must be registered with Gwynedd Council and restrictions apply. A launch fee is payable at the beach just to the south of the campsite. Boats – other than canoes and kayaks – are not allowed in the waters in front of the site. There are designated areas for sailing, windsurfing, powerboats and jet skis. Cars can be taken directly onto the sand. When the tide is out, the beach looks spectacular. Kids can explore the rock pools at low tide. Beach casting is best at night, as things can get busy during the day. Bait up with black lug or crab for bass and flounder.

Facilities include showers, toilets, coin-operated laundry facilities and a children's play area. Several walks over the top of the campsite are good for dogs and there is a holiday park on top of the overhanging cliff face, with good amenities. Dogs are allowed on-site, but there is a charge.

## site info

**OPEN** March to September

**DIRECTIONS** After crossing the Cob at Porthmadog, turn left at The Original Factory Shop in the High Street, and follow the main Morfa Bychan road to the end. At the beach entrance, turn right to the park.

**YEP** Dogs, showers, toilets, tents, caravans, motorhomes, play area, electric

**NO** Shop, bar, restaurant, equipment hire

**ACTIVITIES** Canoe, kayak, fish, swim, sailing dinghy, surf

**RATING** Facilities ★★★★★ Location ★★★★★ Water activities ★★★★★

01766 513919

www.blackrocksands.webs.com

# Llechrwd Riverside Campsite ⑤
## Maentwrog, Gwynedd LL41 4HF

**A shallow, fast-flowing river that flows through Snowdonia into the Irish Sea. The beautiful Vale of Ffestiniog sweeps down from the Crimea Pass, with the Manod and Moelwyn mountains on either side. Tributaries feed into the river Dwyryd as the valley flattens and widens at Llechrwd Farm, before it eventually reaches the harbour at Porthmadog, and estuary of Tremadog Bay.**

All three fields have access to the river. The furthest has a deep waterhole for swimming. Swing tyres hang from trees. For those who bring a canoe, it's possible to navigate the river along the campsite. The adjoining landowner doesn't allow you to pass outside the farm towards the sea and estuary. The river becomes tidal less than one mile from the campsite at the bridge, in Maentwrog, which means no access permission is needed from this point onwards, to the coast. The site owners are lovely and the wife and her daughter are keen canoeists. When I last visited they were setting off on a canoeing trip to the River Wye. Fishing isn't allowed from the campsite, as a neighbouring landowner owns the rights.

Tourers and tents get access to electrical hook-ups. Toilets and showers are excellent and clean. There are riverside and meadow walks, and also a walk to the Rhaedr Cynfal waterfall nearby. The RSPB Glaslyn Osprey viewing site is a 15-minute drive away. The famous Ffestiniog Railway runs from the old slate town at Blaenau Ffestinog, just below the Crimea Pass, down to the harbour at Porthmadog, passing through much of the amazing scenery that surrounds the campsite.

## site info

**OPEN** March to October

**DIRECTIONS** Llechrwd is off the A496, about 1 mile from Maentwrog on the left-hand side of the road, travelling towards Blaenau Ffestiniog.

**YEP** Dogs, showers, toilets, tents, caravans, motorhomes, electric

**NO** Shop, bar, restaurant, play area, equipment hire

**ACTIVITIES** Canoe, kayak, fish (permission needed), swim

**RATING** Facilities ★★★★★ Location ★★★★★ Water activities ★★★★★

01766 590240

www.llechrwd.co.uk

# Glanllyn Lakeside Caravan & Camping Park  ⑥
Llanuwchllyn, Gwynedd LL23 7ST

**Glanllyn offers 16 acres of lakeside camping, mountain views and a vast expanse of water inside the Snowdonia National Park. Bala, the town at the northern end of the water, is a six- or seven-minute drive away.**

The private beach is where campers pitch or launch boats. Those with canoes get up early to navigate Bala's 10-mile perimeter in a day. For the less energetic, sailing out into the middle of the lake is a beautiful way to spend a few hours. Some of the best fishing on the lake is around the edges of the campsite, near where the deep-water shelves begin. Pike, perch, brown trout, roach and eel can be taken. The secret to success is finding the right location, so be prepared to move about and experiment. Live bait works best (red maggot) at dawn and dusk, on a float that keeps your tackle out of the rocks. Lures work for pike, particularly surface plugs. A stream passes around the edge of the campsite. Kids love playing around this water and I'm told trout can be caught, but I've never seen anything other than very small fish.

The River Dee runs through the lake, and this is a fabulous place to explore by canoe, just a few hundred metres from the campsite beach. Trout often feed here. Bala has two sailing clubs and a number of companies provide kayaks, yachts and various other types of boats for rent. Bala Sailing Club is a few minutes away. Bala Adventure and Watersports Centre is a three-mile drive away and offers tuition and equipment hire for sailing, windsurfing, kayaking, white-water rafting, canoeing and mountain biking. Check out www.balawatersports.com for more information.

All the pitches are close to the facilities. Showers and toilets are clean, and the laundry and dishwashing areas are good. Electrical supply is provided to caravans, motorhomes and tents. The camp shop sells basic provisions and maps of local walks, and there's a children's playground. Bala Lake Railway runs along the lake's southern shore. Barmouth's fabulous beaches are a 45-minute drive and Snowdon is one hour away.

## site info

**OPEN** March to October

**DIRECTIONS** Leave Bala town on the A494 to drive along the shore of the lake. Campsite is after about 5 miles, on the left.

**YEP** Dogs, showers, toilets, tents, caravans, motorhomes, play area, electric, shop

**NO** Bar, restaurant, equipment hire

**ACTIVITIES** Canoe, kayak, fish, swim, snorkel, sailing dinghy

**RATING** Facilities ★★★★★ Location ★★★★★ Water activities ★★★★★

01678 540227

www.glanllyn.com

# Shell Island Campsite  7
## Llanbedr, Gwynedd LL45 2PJ

**Shell Island is the UK's largest campsite – but what a treasure. On the north edge of Cardigan Bay, the island used to be a farm and it features in the Doomsday book of 1086. Its 450 acres of grassland, dunes and beach are cut off from the mainland at high tide when the Artro estuary floods.**

Kayak, fish, surf, swim and sail from any of the three bathing beaches. The main beach, which stretches six miles to Barmouth, has some of Wales's highest dunes. The north beach is known as Dinghy Beach as it is the best for launching boats. At the south end of Shell Island, about a mile from the entrance, is St Patrick's Causeway. The bay is perfect for yachting. Abersoch, Pwllheli, Portmadoc, Barmouth and Aberdovey are all within a few hours when sailing. Boats on trailers need to be registered with Gwynedd, Conwy or Anglesey councils. Barmouth Harbour Master can be contacted on 01341 280671. The main channel that leads out from the estuary to the sea to the north can be fished anytime. Bass, flounder, mackerel, dogfish, and skate are all common. Beaches are busy with swimmers during the day, so early morning and dusk are best. Larger fish are sometimes taken on floats around the rocks. The reef at St. Patrick's Causeway runs out for 14 miles and is popular with boat anglers. Peeler crabs can be collected from the rock pools for bait, otherwise there's a fantastic tackle shop on-site where staff offer good advice. Sheltered areas of the estuary, where the River Artro meets the Irish Sea, are fine for canoes and kayaks at high tide. Crabbing with the kids, using a line and bucket, is a lot of fun. Youngsters spend hours around the estuary and harbour quay.

Pitch where you like across 300 acres. Out of season is better, as things get busy in July and August. There are four miles of roads and track, 35 water points and 22 fire extinguisher points. A huge shower and toilet block is right at the centre of the camps. Those who want to camp further afield use their own loos. The Elsan point is next to the main toilet block. Front pitches are exposed, but to the right of the site it's possible to find pitches that are more sheltered by the dunes. The pub, restaurant and snack bar are handy, but busy. Sadly, caravans are not allowed, as the site owners have a camping license only.

## site info

**OPEN** March to November

**DIRECTIONS** Off the A496, west of Llanbhedr, 6 miles north of Barmouth.

**YEP** Dogs, showers, toilets, tents, caravans, motorhomes, electric, shop, bar, restaurant, play area

**NO** Equipment hire, caravans

**ACTIVITIES** Canoe, kayak, fish, swim, snorkel, sailing dinghy, surf

**RATING** Facilities ★★★★★ Location ★★★★★ Water activities ★★★★★

01341 241453

www.shellisland.co.uk

# Fegla Fach Farm Caravan Club CL ⑧
## Arthog, Gwynedd LL39 1BZ

**Paradise is patrolled by a handful of sheep that stand and stare at the mouth of an emerald green river like guardian angels. Fegla's natural harbour is on the south-west corner of Snowdonia National Park, opposite the town of Barmouth, and a few miles from Dolgellau, Tywyn and Aberdovey.**

Pitches at this site offer exclusive access to what I can only describe as the nearest thing I've found to camping heaven. The river is part of a reserve, so boat fishing is banned. Line angling from the beach means fish are on the menu most nights, but check for any changes in the protected status of the water. Small dinghies can be launched from any of the beaches around the shoreline. Swimming and snorkelling are excellent and relatively safe around the shore.

As this is a certificated location, there are only five pitches, although the owners do run another small camping area on the same site. Pitch 2 is one of the best. Water, battery charging and waste disposal is available, but there's no electricity, loos or showers. Day visitors, generators and groundsheets are not accepted. People book up to two years in advance in the warmer seasons. There are often cancellations, so it's always worth trying a last-minute call. The site is sometimes made available in the winter if the ground is dry.

Arthog is renowned as a centre for outdoor activities and the Cregennen Lakes are nearby. The village was once served by rail (the Barmouth to Ruabon service) until it closed in 1964. The line is now a footpath known as the Mawddach Trail, which is popular with walkers and cyclists. Walk over the Barmouth Bridge to the harbour for lunch or breakfast. Pony treks along the main the estuary beaches are available a few minutes away.

## site info

**OPEN** All year (depending on weather)

**DIRECTIONS** Follow the A493 from Dolgellau to Fairbourne. Campsite entrance is about 3 miles before Fairbourne (on the right) beside a green cabin. Enter through the steel farm gate and follow signs.

**YEP** Dogs, tents, caravans, motorhomes

**NO** Electric, shop, bar, restaurant, play area, equipment hire, showers, toilets

**ACTIVITIES** Canoe, kayak, fish, swim, snorkel, sailing dinghy

**RATING** Facilities ★★★★★ Location ★★★★★ Water activities ★★★★★

01341 250442

www.caravanclub.co.uk
Search 'Fegla Fach'

BEST IN Gwynedd

# Cae Du Campsite
## Rhosllefain, Tywyn, Gwynedd LL36 9ND

**Camping by water is the closest I've come to experiencing something 'otherworldly'. Living on a beach or the bank of a stream touches something that feels inexplicably right. If that's a pseudo-religious encounter, then good. Cae Du would be my temple. The campsite sits north of Cardigan Bay, between Tywyn and Fairbourne, on a stone beach. Dolphins come to feed on fish at dusk and dawn.**

Surfing, sailing, swimming and fishing are all easy from the shore. The surf is best two hours either side of the tide. Smart anglers use paternoster rigs to catch rays, bass, and codling, with sand eel, lug, rag and mackerel for bait. Bring two rods, one to cast out a bit further for conger.

Facilities are basic. The toilets needed an upgrade when we visited, and there is no electricity. The showers are coin-operated. Campfires are allowed (the owner and his wife supply the firewood) and the effect is of an almighty nightly ritual – I've never seen anything quite like it. Buy eggs and lamb-and-mint burgers from the farmhouse. Campers occasionally meet up or even sleep in the old on-site barn when the weather turns foul.

Don't miss a chance to travel on the famous steam train that runs seven miles from Tywyn to Abergynolwyn. The Talyllyn Railway line was the first narrow gauge railway in Britain to carry passengers using steam haulage. It's now kept going by a team of volunteers.

## site info

**OPEN** April to October

**DIRECTIONS** Off the A493, 8 miles south of Barmouth and half a mile from Llangelynin, where the road bends away from the coast.

**YEP** Dogs, showers, toilets, tents, caravans, motorhomes

**NO** Electric, shop, bar, restaurant, play area, equipment hire

**ACTIVITIES** Canoe, kayak, fish, swim, snorkel, sailing dinghy, surf

**RATING** Facilities ★★☆☆☆ Location ★★★★★ Water activities ★★★★☆

01766 890345

No website

# Glan y Môr Leisure Park  ⑩
## Clarach Bay, Aberystwyth SY23 3DT

**Touring and camping fields look out across the bay, with the Cambrian Mountains as a backdrop. This is a site exposed to the elements.**

Anglers arrive to catch black bream, bass, turbot, flounder and rays. Sand eel and mackerel work best for bait. From the shore, rocks can cause problems for tackle. Consider float fishing with prawn, particularly to the north of the beach or spinning. This can work at low tide as well as high. Kayak fishing is a good alternative. The Clarach River flows into the bay next to the campsite. The river isn't renowned for fishing, but brown trout can be caught further upstream. Swimming, windsurfing, canoeing and surfing are all popular along the beach. Constitution Hill, just over a mile south, has better surfing for more experienced riders.

The toilets, showers and laundry are clean. Campers can use any of the park's leisure facilities. At the time of our visit, there was free access to the clubhouse and a small charge for the bowling alley, tanning area, sauna and steam room. There is a fee to use the swimming pool. Coin-operated washing and drying facilities are available. The licensed club provides snacks and bar meals, with day and night entertainment. Coastal walks from the campsite over the dunes to Aberystwyth or to Borth, in the north, are excellent. Aberystwyth is a few minutes away and Snowdonia National Park is about 10 minutes away by car. The Vale of Rheidol Railway runs an hour-long train journey, 12 miles from Aberystwyth to Devil's Bridge.

## site info

**OPEN** April to November

**DIRECTIONS** Three miles south of Borth on the B4572 sea-front road. Turn right at Clarach.

**YEP** Dogs, showers, toilets, tents, caravans, motorhomes, electric, shop, bar, restaurant, play area, equipment hire

**NO** -

**ACTIVITIES** Canoe, kayak, fish, swim, sailing dinghy, surf

**RATING** Facilities ★★★★★ Location ★★★★★ Water activities ★★★★★

01970 828900

www.sunbourne.co.uk/parks/

# Pengarreg Caravan & Camping Park  ⑪
## Llanrhystud, Aberystwyth SY23 5DH

This place is all about surfing and fishing. But be warned – there are seals. It's quite a sight watching rookie boarders make a dash for the shore when they realise large 'sea creatures' are hunting around them. In reality, there's little to fear from the wildlife, but they can give you a fright if you're not expecting to meet them. Pengarreg is on a black stone beach at Llanrhystud, surrounded by fine walking country. Sands are just 20 minutes away at New Quay village and Aberystwyth. Aberaeron is a harbour town six miles south.

The best waves are around the incoming tide on a good wind. But care is needed, as rocks and boulders are just below the waterline, and there are strong currents all around. Dinghies and canoes can be launched from the slipway right at the centre of the camping field. Either the boat ramp or the beach is good for casting (see page 28 for more information). The River Wyre runs next to the caravan park, with a mile of private trout and sea trout fishing. Sea trips are available from any of the neighbouring harbours. Swimmers need to take care.

Most of the touring pitches are in the second row back from the beach, with the shore side generally taken by seasonals. Back pitches are fine, and they have easy access to the walks over the hills. Toilets are modern, with free hot and cold showers, and dishwashing facilities. Washing machines and dryers are in the laundry room. The general store stocks camping and food essentials. Other facilities include a kids' playground, a clubhouse with a bar, an entertainment room and an outside adventure playground – it's well away from the campsite, so noise is minimal.

## site info

**OPEN** March to December

**DIRECTIONS** Just off the A487 Aberystwyth to Cardigan road in the village of Llanrhystud, opposite the service station, 9 miles south of Aberystwyth.

**YEP** Dogs, showers, toilets, tents, caravans, motorhomes, electric, shop, bar, restaurant, play area

**NO** Equipment hire

**ACTIVITIES** Canoe, kayak, fish, swim, sailing dinghy, surf

**RATING** Facilities ★★★★★ Location ★★★★★ Water activities ★★★★★

01974 202247

www.utowcaravans.co.uk/pengarreg. html

BEST IN
Ceredigion

# Morfa Farm Caravan Park  ⑫
Cardigan Bay, Llanrhystud SY23 5BU

**Trout fishing on a river in Cardigan Bay, camping on a stony shore and lighting communal beach fires by night. Morfa Farm Caravan Park is nine miles from the towns of Aberaeron and Aberystwyth.**

The owners – a friendly and helpful family – hold angling rights to a three-quarter-mile stretch along the River Wyre. The river passes east through Llanrhystud and Llangwyryfon, in the county of Ceredigion, before turning south through Lledrod. Offshore there's fishing for whiting, flatfish and mackerel. Dogfish are common. Although sold in England as rock salmon, most anglers seem to throw them back. Bass, mullet and cod feed here in the winter. Kids enjoy splashing and paddling about in the river where it meets the Irish Sea. For kayakers, there are some beautiful coves to discover along Cardigan Bay. A slipway makes launching larger boats easy. The beach is also good swimming and surfing.

Pitches riverside have no electricity, but the back rows do. Toilets, showers and other basic amenities are all good. Public footpaths run along the coast and up the mountainside. This is a good site for birdwatchers, as red kite and choughs are regular visitors.

The towns of Aberaeron and Aberystwyth are 15 minutes away. Aberaeron is famous for its honey mustard, and ice cream. Fishguard port is an hour away by car, and ferries to Rosslare, Ireland, leave from there every day.

## site info

**OPEN** March to October

**DIRECTIONS** Take the A487 from Aberystwyth towards Aberaeron. After passing through the village of Llanrhystud, bear right at the petrol station and follow the left road leading to the beach. The caravan park is the last right turn before the beach.

**YEP** Dogs, showers, toilets, tents, caravans, motorhomes, electric, shop

**NO** Bar, restaurant, play area, equipment hire

**ACTIVITIES** Canoe, kayak, fish, swim, sailing dinghy, surf

**RATING** Facilities ★★★★★ Location: ★★★★★ Water activities ★★★★★

01974 202253

www.morfa.net

# Canalside Caravan & Camping ❶

31 Grindley Brook, Whitchurch, Shropshire SY13 4QJ

**Famous locks are the attraction at this adult-only site on the Llangollen Canal. Fishing and canoeing are allowed on the canal with permits. It's possible to paddle from Grindley Brook to Ellesmere, just over 10 miles away. Angling is also good in ponds situated about the campsite, close to the tenting area.**

More than 20 pitches come with electrical supply and TV points, and there are eight pitches for tents. Hot showers, a toilet block, a washing-up area, laundry room and fridge-freezer are all available. The Grindley Brook staircase of locks is a five-minute walk away (see page 112). A pub, shop and garage are all close by. The market town of Whitchurch is a 30-minute walk and the camp is next to the Sandstone Trail.

# site info

**OPEN** March to October

**DIRECTIONS** Drive towards Whitchurch on the A41 from Chester. On entering Grindley Brook, pass a 40-mph sign, and the site is on the left, opposite the Horse and Jockey pub car park.

**YEP** Dogs, showers, toilets, tents, caravans, motorhomes, electric

**NO** Children, shop, bar, restaurant, play area

**ACTIVITIES** Canoe, kayak, fish

**RATING** Facilities ★★★★★ Location ★★★★★ Water activities ★★★★★

01948 663284

www.canalsidecaravansite.20m.com

# Grindley Brook Wharf Caravan & Campsite
Whitchurch, Shropshire SY13 4QH

**Lockside on the Llangollen Canal is the watery equivalent of Birmingham's Spaghetti Junction at rush hour. Wharf Campsite is at the top of a series of six locks in the village of Grindley Brook, on the Cheshire-Shropshire and Welsh-English borders. Canalside camping rarely gets as enjoyable as this.**

Roach, rudd, perch, carp, tench, gudgeon and pike are caught in the canal (a British Waterways permit is needed). Boats can be launched, but as the Grindley Brook staircase becomes a bottleneck from Easter onwards, finding a quiet section of water can be a problem.

Most of the Llangollen Canal's 41 miles can be navigated by canoe or kayak. The canal leaves the Shropshire Union Canal just north of Nantwich, in Cheshire, and ends at the River Dee, in Llangollen. From the campsite, paddle to the left away from the lock towards Whitchurch, a mile away. Cole Meres is 11 miles, followed by Blake Mere, and then the market town of Ellesmere. Locks along this canal are considered, in canal terms, among the wonders of the world – this is British engineering at its best.

Toilets and showers are basic but clean. Pitches have access to electricity. Wardens are helpful and friendly. The towpath is on the opposite side of the canal, so walkers and cyclists don't encroach too much on camp privacy. Boats and barges pass the locks three at a time in either direction during high season, with queues sometimes stretching for up to half a mile past the campsite. Watching the skippers attempting to navigate the system makes for good daytime entertainment. The Lockside store has a coffee shop and internet access, and stocks groceries, boat and camping gear and alcohol. Several good pubs in the immediate area are worth visiting. Grindley Brook village is the starting point for several long-distance walks, which include the Maelor Way, Shropshire Way, Marches Way, South Cheshire Way and the Sandstone Trail. Whitchurch town is less than two miles away.

## site info

**OPEN** April to October

**DIRECTIONS** Drive towards Chester on the A41 from Whitchurch. Just before Grindley Brook, look for the large yellow house on the left (Grindley Brook House). The camp entrance is just past the house on the left.

**YEP** Dogs, electric, showers, toilets, caravans, motorhomes (shop, restaurant next to the site)

**NO** Tents, play area, equipment hire, bar

**ACTIVITIES** Canoe, kayak, fish

**RATING** Facilities ★★★★★ Location ★★★★★ Water activities ★★★★★

01948 664003

No website

# Whitchurch Marina

Wrexham Road, Whitchurch, Shropshire SY13 3AA

**Camping in a service station doesn't fill me with excitement – but Whitchurch Marina is a fuel stop with character, and a base to explore Shrewsbury, Wrexham and Chester.**

Fishing and boating are the best way to enjoy the site. Those without canoes or kayaks can hire a barge, but only for a minimum of seven days. Whitchurch Marina provides access to cruising through Ellesmere and Chirk to Llangollen, via the famous Pontcysyllte Aqueduct, a World Heritage site. In the other direction, it's possible to go north on the Shropshire Union canal toward Chester until you reach the River Mersey at Ellesmere Port.

There are a handful of pitches (hardstanding or grass), with a shower and toilet block, a washroom, waste disposal, on-site shop and Wi-Fi. The staff are helpful but busy. The on-site shop sells maps, guides, ice creams, soft drinks and deck gear for narrow boats and other craft. Watch the passing barges from the campsite, amongst the cows who keep their heads down and focus on eating.

Whitchurch is within walking distance, and has some decent pubs, restaurants, a swimming pool and a golf course. Jubilee Park, in Whitchurch, is the starting point for five long-distance walks, including the Shropshire Way. Ramble from here down to staircase locks at Grindley Brook, a mile or so out of town, and then back to the marina.

## site info

**OPEN** All year

**DIRECTIONS** Leave the A41 at Whitchurch, turning west onto the A525. The campsite entrance is on the right.

**YEP** Dogs, showers, toilets, tents, caravans, motorhomes, equipment hire, electric, shop

**NO** Bar, restaurant, play area

**ACTIVITIES** Canoe, kayak, fish

**RATING** Facilities ★★★★★ Location ★★★★★ Water activities ★★★★★

01948 662 012

www.whitchurchmarina.com

# Severn House Campsite ④
## Shrewsbury, Shropshire SY4 1ED

**Severn House was built 400 years ago as a pub and stables for weary travellers, traders and the horses that pulled barges. The drive in front of the house is the old A5. Everything here is relaxed, apart from the river, which is in something of a rush. Medieval Shrewsbury, built within a loop of the river, is 10 minutes away.**

Things here today are mostly about fishing and leisure boating. Canoeists take a break or camp overnight as part of their river-tour expeditions. Launching is free if you are staying on-site, but there's a small charge for fishing. Anglers make up the on-site community by day. Large barbel and chub are mostly caught on pellets, paste and large chunks of luncheon meat. Pre-baiting can work well in areas where the water flow is slower. The riverbank is steep, so take care getting down.

Of the 30 pitches, most come with electrical supply. Hot showers and toilets are good and the owners are friendly. The campsite shop sells BBQ sausages, burgers and bacon sourced from a farm at Market Drayton. Milk, tea and eggs are also available. Walks are possible across the surrounding countryside. The Wingfield Arms pub is within 200 metres on the other side of the river, over the bridge. Shrewsbury has more than 600 listed buildings to explore. Nesscliffe Country Park, home of Wild Humphrey Kynaston, known as 'Shropshire's Robin Hood', is about a 10-minute drive away.

## site info

**OPEN** April to October

**DIRECTIONS** Leave the A5 north west of Shrewsbury onto the B3480. The campsite is on the left, just before the road bridge across the River Severn.

**YEP** Dogs, showers, toilets, tents, caravans, motorhomes, electric

**NO** Shop, bar, restaurant, play area, equipment hire

**ACTIVITIES** Canoe, kayak, fish

**RATING** Facilities ★★★★★ Location ★★★★★ Water activities ★★★★★

01743 850229

www.severnhousecampsite.co.uk

BEST IN Shropshire

# The Anchor Inn ⑤
## Old Lea, High Offley, Staffordshire ST20 0NG

**Flowers, pastel colours, a canal and a pub, four miles from Newport. The same family has run the Anchor Inn for more than 100 years. The owner is friendly, and runs a tight ship around her tiny home, which seems stuck in a cosy time warp.**

Sixty-six miles of canal are navigable by canoe or kayak. This southern section of the Shropshire Union Canal was created towards the end of canal age, when British engineering was at its best. Unlike the earlier winding canals, The Shroppie holds her line through hills and valleys. Roach, perch, chub, pike and gudgeon can be fished once you have bought a permit.

Thirteen hook-up pitches are available on the campsite, five of which are for Caravan Club members. A chemical waste disposal is provided, but no showers or hot water. Warning signs posted by the owners forbid rogue parking and dogs. It's a shame there's no view of the canal, which is obscured by a large hedge, but that is good excuse to buy a drink and sit in the beer garden, which overlooks the water and the passing river traffic. Beer is still brought up from the cellar in jugs, which adds to the old-world feel and when you're sitting in the garden, it's easy to imagine the scene here more than a century ago. Punters are mostly made up of boaters who stop over and the odd local. Sadly, the pub doesn't serve food, but there's another at Norbury Junction, two miles along the canal, that does. There are walks in both directions along the canal.

**BEST IN Staffordshire**

## site info

**OPEN** Easter to October

**DIRECTIONS** Leave the M6 at junction 14. Take the A5013 towards Eccleshall. Turn left onto the B5405 towards Woodseaves at Great Bridgeford. At the end of the road, turn right onto the A519. Turn left onto High Offley Road, then past the church turn left into Peggs Lane. The Anchor Inn is on the left over Canal Bridge.

**YEP** Dogs, tents, caravans, motorhomes, pub

**NO** Electric, shop, restaurant, play area, equipment hire, showers, toilets

**ACTIVITIES** Canoe, kayak, fish

**RATING** Facilities ★★★★★ Location ★★★★★ Water activities ★★★★★

01785 284569

No website

# Pillaton Hall Farm
## Penkridge, Staffordshire ST19 5RZ

**This is diversification at its best – a professional fishery that accommodates campers on a working farm. Pillaton Hall Farm is set in the Staffordshire countryside, overlooking 3,000 acres of heath land known as Cannock Chase. The Staffordshire and Worcestershire Canal is within walking distance at Penkridge.**

Four large pools are stocked with everything from skimmer bream to 20-pound carp, roach, eels and golden orfe. Fishing is between dawn and dusk. The Cherry Pool, at the site entrance, was built in the 1960s as a farm reservoir, and drops to 5 metres towards the car-park end. A stream enters the water from the other end. The Dip is the largest pool, with an island in the middle, making it ideal for feeders. Its shallow edges mean it's also the safest spot for kids. The Cherry Pool is the only pond that's always open. Other pools are only open if there are no matches on. Ian's Fishing Shop, at Penkridge, offers good advice on bait and techniques.

A vast amount of space is given over to tourers around the water's edge – more than 140 pitches have been laid out in the back of this working farm. Electrical points can be quite a distance, which means bringing a cable extension or hiring one for a few pounds. Some families were worried that the children's play area was too close to one of the fishing lakes, but I anticipate that it will get fenced off before long. Hot showers are clean and have shower-gel dispensers.

Walking, pony trekking or mountain biking are available in the surrounding Chase area. Penkridge market is worth a visit. Indian and Chinese takeaways deliver to the campsite. There are several pubs at Penkridge.

## site info

**OPEN** April to October

**DIRECTIONS** Take the B5012 out of Penkridge, pass under the M6 and follow the road around the bend. Pillaton Hall Farm is next turning on the left.

**YEP** Dogs, showers, toilets, tents, caravans, motorhomes, play area, electric

**NO** Shop, bar, restaurant, equipment hire

**ACTIVITIES** Fish

**RATING** Facilities ★★★★★ Location ★★★★★ Water activities ★★★★★

01785 715177

www.pillatonpools.co.uk

## Bosworth Water Trust  7
Nuneaton, Warwickshire CV13 6PD

**It all began here, with our first camping holiday by water in 2003. The current owners discovered underwater boreholes on farmland less than a mile outside Market Bosworth and dug out two lakes. They had a passion for boats, and by creating their own water park they followed their dream and spawned a business.**

This remains as good as any site I've come across. A shallow, safe stretch of water, where sailing dinghies, powerboats, rowing boats and pedalos can be hired out. Bosworth Water Trust is an approved training centre and offers courses in all of the above. Kids' clubs are available on Saturday, with trainers offering two-hour sessions on the water. Campers can use their own craft on the lake for a small charge, subject to providing an insurance certificate. Triathletes hold swimming training on the water here several times a week. The fishing here is incredibly easy and fun for all ages. Huge carp swim lazily about the place, as if they're in an aqua-retirement home. A 28-pound common carp was caught in 2008. Tench, roach, bream, perch, chub and trout are caught on maggots, pellets, spam and sweetcorn. The lake fishing is open to the public – campers pay half price for a day ticket. Young kids can buy pellets from the shop to feed hundreds of giant carp at the angling-free zone, next to the wooden pier, near the campsite entrance.

There are more than 50 pitches, for caravans, tents and motorhomes. The best are right next to the small beach and can be booked in advance. During the height of the season, these areas can become very busy and some campers prefer to book a pitch further back. Electricity is available. Toilets and showers are good. It's a joy to sit outside the licensed café on a summer's evening to watch the sun set behind the lake. Ashby Canal is a few hundred yards' walk from the park, along the adjoining country lane. It's possible to fish or canoe on the canal. Almost a decade on, we've discovered and stayed at hundreds of great alternatives to Bosworth but this place still takes some beating.

BEST IN
Warwickshire

# site info

**OPEN** All year

**DIRECTIONS** On the B585, just west of Market Bosworth, in Warwickshire.

**YEP** Dogs, showers, toilets, tents, caravans, motorhomes, electric, shop, bar, restaurant, play area, equipment hire

**NO** -

**ACTIVITIES** Canoe, kayak, fish, swim, sailing dinghy

**RATING** Facilities ★★★★★ Location ★★★★★ Water activities ★★★★★

01455 291876

www.bosworthwatertrust.co.uk

# Lickhill Manor Caravan Park ⑧
## Stourport-on-Severn, Worcestershire DY13 8RL

**My favourite site in Worcestershire is big, beautiful and clean. More than 60 acres of farmland surround the 17th-century manor house on the River Severn. Stourport-on-Severn is a 15-minute stroll along the river, or a 30-minute paddle by canoe. Walk in the opposite direction for about an hour to Bewdley.**

Two vast meadows lead down to the chocolate-coloured Severn. It's not a river renowned for its calm, but there is stillness here. Almost one mile of river frontage is split between permanent mooring and wooden platforms for fishing. Large barbel, chub, roach, perch and tench can be caught. Anglers have success with worms, maggots, spinners and pellets. Fishing permits, valid for one week, are available from reception for a small fee. The riverbank is steep and hazardous in places, but an earth slipway makes launching dinghies and canoes easy.

The river's highest reaches are at Pool Quay, in Welshpool, Powys, 81 miles away. Most of the water is defined as Grade 1 with only occasional simple rapids, but some places can prove hazardous. Take advice if setting out for a long trip. A British Waterways Board license is needed for the 45 miles between Stourport and Gloucester. Navigation is totally free from Stourport to Pool Quay. Apart from Shrewsbury Weir and the rapids at Jackfield and Eymore, it's relatively hazard-free. The Severn becomes tidal from Tewkesbury, as it gets closer to the Bristol Channel.

The 300 pitches and 68 electrical points put this at the larger end of camping parks, but there's lots of space. Toilets and showers cope with the peak summer traffic and staff are always helpful. Ducks, goats and chickens roam about the place. Takeaways can be delivered on-site. The boat hire, pubs, cafés and shops are excellent at Stourport-on-Severn. The River Severn, the River Stour, and the Staffordshire and Worcestershire Canal surround the town to create a unique setting in the Severn Valley. Walking is quicker than driving and saves the hassle of parking.

BEST IN
Worcestershire

## site info

**OPEN** All year

**DIRECTIONS** One mile from Stourport. Follow signposts for the park from the one-way system.

**YEP** Dogs, showers, toilets, tents, caravans, motorhomes

**NO** Electric, shop, bar, restaurant, play area, equipment hire

**ACTIVITIES** Canoe, kayak, fish, swim, snorkel, sailing dinghy

**RATING** Facilities ★★★★★ Location ★★★★★ Water activities ★★★★★

01299 871041

www.lickhillmanor.co.uk

# Island Meadow Caravan Park

Henley-in-Arden, Warwickshire B95 6JP

**Old and young; then and now; slow and fast – the setting alone has it all. A furious stream flows on one side, while the River Alne meanders on the other. Both watercourses create a seven-acre island retreat to escape from it all. The churchyard of St John's, a short walk away, is where Shakespeare's parents were married.**

Mature trees line the riverbanks. An old millpond with a weir provides free coarse fishing. Unlike some other water sites, kids are relatively safe here, as the River Alne is mostly shallow along this stretch. Fishermen can get a tad annoyed with the kids who splash about, but this is the sort of place the young ones will remember forever – a real-life Enid Blyton adventure where netting tiddlers, paddling and jumping about on toy inflatables is all part of the fun. A deep waterhole close to the weir is for older kids and adults. Canoeing is only possible from the campsite when the river is high. There are places to launch a little further downstream or beyond the weir.

A family runs the site. Their spaniel can be grumpy, but he's all bark and no bite. Statics, tourers, campervans and tents are accommodated, all with electrical supply, if needed. Tourers have access to 24 pitches, while tents have The Orchard, to the front of the Mill House and the garden. The only real noise at the site is the millrace, gushing day and night, behind the toilet blocks and showers. Facilities include a washing-up area, with a washing machine, and a children's play area. The small shop stocks basics, including fresh bread and cakes. Otters are sometimes seen along the river, and the owners have recently installed an artificial otter holt. There are loads of good walks from the site into the countryside. It's a nice, easy stroll to the 15th-century Kings Head Inn, at Aston Cantlow, or across the Mill Meadow to St John's churchyard. Park and Ride for Stratford-upon-Avon is 15 minutes by car. Warwick and the Cotswolds are nearby, too.

## site info

**OPEN** March to October

**DIRECTIONS** On the A46, between Stratford-upon-Avon and Alcester, or from the A3400 at Wootton Wawen, follow the signs for Aston Cantlow. Turn into Mill Lane, either off Brook Road or Wilmcote Lane. Site is on the right.

**YEP** Dogs, showers, toilets, tents, caravans, motorhomes, electric, shop, play area

**NO** Bar, restaurant, equipment hire

**ACTIVITIES** Canoe, kayak, fish, swim

**RATING** Facilities ★★★★★ Location ★★★★★ Water activities ★★★★★

01789 488 273

www.islandmeadowcaravanpark.co.uk

# Tresseck Campsite (10)
## Hoarwithy, Hereford HR2 6QJ

**Tresseck is situated down a narrow track, in the village of Hoarwithy, mid-way between the city of Hereford and the market town of Ross-on-Wye. Wooden steps lead down from the riverbank to the water, where it's possible to swim or launch a canoe.**

The site is a popular stopover for canoeists and kayakers passing along the river. Ross-on-Wye can be reached by paddle in about four hours, and Hereford in six. There are several canoe hire centres in the area. For more information and for latest information on river access at Tresseck, call 01432 840235. The water here is clean and excellent for swimming, but care is needed after heavy rain when the river flow becomes dangerously fast. Fishing rights are granted along about 250 metres of the River Wye and there is a small daily fee for anglers. Fish feed on large numbers of damselflies here during the late summer months.

Pitches are in old river meadow, and there's plenty of room, but for tents only. The council has refused to grant permission for caravans and motorhomes. Facilities include running water and portable loos. Campfires are allowed and the owner sells wood to those who don't bring their own. The New Harp Inn, a few minutes' walk away, serves food. A swimming pool in Ross-on-Wye is handy if you don't fancy taking the plunge in the river.

## site info

**OPEN** April to October

**DIRECTIONS** Follow the A49 south from Hereford through Much Birch. Take the next left (signposted Hoarwithy). Find The New Harp Inn in Hoarwithy and the campsite is just to the left.

**YEP** Dogs, toilets, tents, showers, electric

**NO** Shop, bar, restaurant, play area, equipment hire, caravans, motorhomes

**ACTIVITIES** Canoe, kayak, fish, swim

**RATING** Facilities ★★★★★ Location ★★★★★ Water activities ★★★★★

01432 840235

www.tresseckcampsite.co.uk

# Lucksall Touring & Camping Park (11)
## Mordiford, Herefordshire HR1 4LP

**Lucksall Park is bordered by 110 acres of park and woodland along one of the quietest sections of the Wye. Wonderful wardens and fabulous canoeing make it a special place to holiday. This is among the Caravan Club's finest sites, five miles from the cathedral city of Hereford and nine miles from Ross-on-Wye.**

Get up early, and it's possible to paddle to Hereford, via Mordiford, the village of Holme Lacy and eventually past the cathedral. The Bunch of Carrots pub, just before Hereford, at Hampton Bishop, serves decent food. Paddling in the other direction, you can get to Hoarwithy Bridge and back in a day, via the villages of Fownhope and Ballingham. Camping is available just after the bridge if you want to stay overnight. Take care with kids, as the Lucksall riverbank is a bit steep in places. Two canoe launches, either end of the camp, provide easy access. Canadian-style canoes are for hire on-site. Otters are seen along this stretch of the river. A tackle shop on-site offers angling advice and permits. Barbel and chub are common. Halibut pellets do well, especially when using swim feeders to spread ground bait. A combination of hemp and red maggot will work fine, too.

Many pitches are on the grass next to the river, although not all have river access, so check first if that's what you want. Washing and shower blocks are super-clean. The camp shop and café are reasonably priced with a complimentary pot of tea on arrival, which is a very nice touch. Just outside the campsite entrance are miles of forest track for rambling, cycling and dig walks. Pick up free maps from the campsite reception. Pubs and shops are within a mile and a half, although the country road can be dangerous if walking back at night, so take care. Buses stop outside the main entrance for Hereford, and some will transport canoes.

## site info

**OPEN** March to November

**DIRECTIONS** Just off the B4224, less than 5 miles south east of Hereford. Just south of the B3449, turn right if heading south, towards Ross-on-Wye.

**YEP** Dogs, showers, toilets, tents, caravans, motorhomes, electric, shop, restaurant, play area, equipment hire

**NO** -

**ACTIVITIES** Canoe, kayak, fish, swim

**RATING** Facilities ★★★★★ Location ★★★★★ Water activities ★★★★★

01432 870213

www.lucksallpark.co.uk

BEST IN Herefordshire

# Eastnor Castle 12
## Ledbury, Herefordshire HR8 1RL

**Camping in a deer park next to a fishing lake in the shadow of a medieval castle is something a bit special. The castle has been a family home for nearly 200 years, and is maintained by the Hervey-Bathursts with grants from English Heritage.**

Camping in the grounds comes with views of the castle, the Malvern Hills and the Eastnor Lake – stocked with carp, perch, roach and rudd. There is a charge for fishing, either per person or for a family. The water bailiff is Ian, and his home number is 01531 634280. Expect fish of up to 15 pounds in weight.

There are no facilities here except water and chemical waste disposal, but that's all part of the appeal. No campfires permitted, but raised BBQs are allowed and wood can be collected. You can pitch anywhere, which is my favourite kind of camping. The campground gently slopes down towards the lake but flat areas can be found. Tents and caravans can only stay for a maximum of seven consecutive nights, unless by special arrangement.

The views are stunning and there are wonderful old oak trees. The park is designated an Area of Outstanding Natural Beauty and a Site of Special Scientific Interest. Deer have been fenced out because of the damage they cause, although they can still be seen grazing. Campers get a half-price family ticket for entry to Eastnor Castle, which provides excellent entertainment. Annual events held in the deer park include open-air concerts, fun runs, a fireworks championship, and 24-hour mountain-bike endurance races. Ledbury town is nearby and dates back to 690 AD.

## site info

**OPEN** March to October

**DIRECTIONS** On the A438 Tewkesbury Road, 2½ miles east of Ledbury, in Eastnor Deer Park.

**YEP** Dogs, chemical waste, fresh water, tents, caravans, motorhomes

**NO** Electric, shop, bar, restaurant, play area, equipment hire, showers, toilets

**ACTIVITIES** fish

**RATING** Facilities ★★★★★ Location ★★★★★ Water activities ★★★★★

01531 633160

www.eastnorcastle.com.caravanning.aspx

# Croft Farm Water Park 13

Tewkesbury, Gloucestershire GL20 7EE

**Campers get a combination of watersports and great facilities in the Avon Valley, just a few minutes from Tewkesbury. A footpath around the lake leads to a neighbouring meadow and the river. Croft Farm is a Royal Yachting Association Training Centre, and offers courses for all ages in sailing, kayaking, canoeing and even raft building. Bring your own equipment (insurance is needed) or hire.**

Fishing is free and a private slipway for motorised craft was built onto the river in 2011. The watersports centre was rebuilt in 2011 with a new shop, function room and changing rooms next to the water. The lake is small enough for teaching, but large enough for more skilful sailors and windsurfers to have fun. Sailing, windsurfing, canoeing and fishing are all good. Launching anywhere around the lake is easy.

A mixture of grass and hard-standing pitches cater for caravans, motorhomes and tents. Some areas around the lake are reserved for seasonal pitches, but there's space for campers arriving for a day or two. Lakeside pitches are best, although they can sometimes be tighter width-wise than those further back. The owners here are helpful and there are incredibly few rules (which we like). Campers get a key fob for gate access, loos and showers. Facilities include a laundry room, dishwashing sinks, a log-cabin club house and gym. The Lakeside café and bar are open through the day and into the evening. Children have an outdoor and indoor play area, space to cycle around the site and the opportunity to take part in the watersports.

The health and fitness centre is managed as a separate business serving the local community, but visitors staying on-site can join as day members. A festival is held each year – visit www.lakefest.co.uk for more information. The Cross Keys pub across the road serves real ales and good food. Tewkesbury hosts Europe's largest battle re-enactment and fair in July, and also a Water Festival. There is some doubt about its future because of funding and recent floods have seen the annual event cancelled. The Cotswolds, Malverns, Bredon Hill and the Forest of Dean are nearby.

BEST IN Gloucestershire

## site info

**OPEN** March to November

**DIRECTIONS** Head east out of Tewkesbury on the B4080 towards Bredon. After a mile and a half you will see the park signs on the left-hand side. The site is almost opposite the Cross Keys Inn.

**YEP** Dogs, showers, toilets, tents, caravans, motorhomes, electric, shop, bar, restaurant, play area, equipment hire

**NO** -

**ACTIVITIES** Canoe, kayak, fish, sailing dinghy

**RATING** Facilities ★★★★★ Location ★★★★★ Water activities ★★★★★

01684 772321

www.croftfarmleisure.co.uk

# Winchcombe Camping & Caravanning Club Site

Brooklands Farm, Alderton, Gloucestershire GL20 8NX

**Pitches around a small fishing lake, run by friendly, diligent wardens, in the Cotswolds. Tewkesbury's timber-framed buildings on the River Avon are less than a 10-minute drive away. Cheltenham, to the south west, hosts jazz and literature festivals.**

Ducks add to the ambience of calm as they amble from pitch to pitch looking for grubs and handouts. Anglers fish for carp and chub from wooden swims set around the edge of a well-stocked lake. Carp as large as eight pounds are regularly caught. Spam works best. There are very few rules, apart from a strange one: no maggots. I was told that several years ago a rogue angler carelessly tossed some unused bait on the ground. A camper arrived and unknowingly pitched an awning over the maggots, which several days later hatched into flies and ruined the family's holiday. I'm not entirely sure about the veracity of the story (I haven't checked it officially), but it's an interesting tale.

Many of the 90 pitches surround the circle of the lake, although not all get a view, as bushes and fruit trees shelter much of the water. Wardens are knowledgeable and friendly and keep the site spotless. Showers and loos are clean. Electricity is provided with the pitch fee. Wi-Fi is available, but doesn't cover the entire camp. The lake has open access to the front, but is gated and fenced at the back for families with young children. A small ball area in the children's play area is also a handy extra for families. The site shop sells local free-range eggs and apple juice from a nearby farm. Hayles Fruit Farm produces and stocks a range of fruit juices and has an outlet in Winchcombe. The Gardeners Arms is the nearest pub, but there are at least four more nearby. A fish-and-chip van visits twice a week. The village of Alderton is nearby.

## site info

**OPEN** March to January

**DIRECTIONS** Off the B4077, east of Tewkesbury, 1.5 miles on the right before Shetcombe Wood.

**YEP** Dogs, showers, toilets, tents, caravans, motorhomes, electric, shop, play area

**NO** Bar, restaurant, equipment hire

**ACTIVITIES** Fish

**RATING** Facilities ★★★★★ Location ★★★★★ Water activities ★★★★★

01242 620259

www.campingandcaravanningclub.co.uk/winchcombe

# Weir Meadow Park  15

Lower Leys, Evesham, Worcestershire WR11 3AA

**Known as 'Shakespeare's Avon' or 'the Stratford Avon', the famous river dominates this park. The Weir is the campsite's centre, a navigational point and a roost for scores of Brent Geese. Weir Meadow Park is in the market town of Evesham, with easy access to the Vale of Evesham and the Cotswolds.**

Sailing is available from a ramp just beside the campsite. The Lower Avon meanders away from the weir and campsite for about three miles. The Upper stretch, above the Weir, was once the haunt of the Evesham Sailing Club. Sadly, the club closed in 2010 because of a lack of members. It may still be possible to launch from the site, which is council-owned (check with Evesham Council).

The water here is wide and deep. Fishing is available from 40 pegs. Permits are valid from dawn till dusk. Expect to catch barbel, zander, pike and perch. A slipway provides access to the river for canoes and kayaks and there are boat moorings available. Boaters need to buy a license from the lock offices to use the river. Evesham hosts a river festival in July each year – for more information go to www.eveshamriverfestival.co.uk

Twenty-four pitches are available from March to December. The showers are spotless, and the site is well looked after, with a laundry room, picnic area and barbecue facilities. There are lots of shops and restaurants in Evesham and Stratford-upon-Avon is 20 miles away.

# site info

**OPEN** March to December

**DIRECTIONS** Head for Port Street in Evesham. Turn into Burford Road, by the Regal Cinema. Take the first left in Burford Road into Lower Leys. The park is at the bottom of the road on the right.

**YEP** Dogs, showers, toilets, caravans, motorhomes, electric

**NO** Tents, shop, bar, restaurant, play area, equipment hire

**ACTIVITIES** Canoe, kayak, sailing dinghy, fish

**RATING** Facilities ★★★★★ Location ★★★★★ Water activities ★★★★★

01386 442417

www.allenscaravans.com/holiday-home-parks/findapark/weir-meadow

# Friars Court 16

Clanfield, Oxfordshire OX18 2SU

**Charles Willmer runs this meadow island, surrounded by a non-tidal section of the River Thames. It represents basic camping at its best, in one of the finest canoeing areas in England, between the village of Clanfield and the market town of Faringdon.**

Coarse fishing is allowed from June 16 onwards, but only with a local permit. The river can be a bit weedy at times and there's often a family of swans in and around, pestering for food, although they do add to the charm. Decent-sized pike and chub swim below the surface. An Environment Agency license is needed for the trapping of American Signal (non-native) crayfish. Canoeists sometimes park in the adjoining pub car park to access the river, although it's easy to launch directly from the pitches, with good paddling in both directions. The pub provides a fine place to relax and meet people after a long day out on the river or in the field.

Four acres of campsite accommodate five vans in this Caravan Club certified location. Boats use the island meadow for moorings. A second meadow was formerly a Rally Field by the pub for up to 60 caravans, but new owners have suggested this may not continue. Basic amenities for water, litter and a sanitation point are provided. Generators are not allowed and there's no electricity.

The Friars Court house is nearby and has historic links to The Knights Hospitaller, a powerful Christian order that once owned land throughout Oxfordshire. The buildings at Friars Court date back to 1142 and the establishment of the first 'Hospitaller' in Oxfordshire by the Knights Templar Order of St John of Jerusalem. Faringdon is a peaceful town worth a visit. Nearby Faringdon House is renowned for its strange custom of dyeing pigeons.

## site info

**OPEN** March to October, depending on weather

**DIRECTIONS** Where the A4095 crosses the River Thames, between Clanfield and Faringdon.

**YEP** Dogs, tents, caravans, motorhomes

**NO** Electric, shop, bar, restaurant, play area, equipment hire, showers, toilets

**ACTIVITIES** Canoe, kayak, fish

**RATING** Facilities ★★★★★ Location ★★★★★ Water activities ★★★★★

01367 810206

www.friarscourt.com

BEST IN Oxfordshire

# Bridge House Caravan Site
## Abingdon, Oxfordshire OX14 3EH

**Despite our clash with the 'security guards' on arrival, this is a wonderful site. Swans, geese and ducks patrol the grounds like a gang of aggressive doormen. There's an ancient feel about the camp that I like. Abingdon-on-Thames holds claim to being one of Britain's oldest occupied towns, dating back 6,000 years.**

Thames river traffic makes for fine amusement, although it's not so good for angling. We caught very little between the hours of 9.30 am and 5.45 pm, so decided to fish early and late, and hooked some good-sized carp with halibut pellets. Barbel, chub, pike and roach are common here, too. It's possible to moor a boat beside your own pitch.

The site is popular for canoeists, and some were allowed to launch from the riverbank even though they were not camping. Abingdon Weir, with its steep, high concrete ramp, is to the east of the town centre and attracts members of the local canoe club. A beautiful day's canoe is possible from Abingdon to Wallingford, a stretch of 13 miles and four locks. Canoes sometimes stop over at Benson (see page 134) and then go 10 miles further upriver the next day, to Pangbourne. The Thames is the longest river in England, covering more than 200 miles through Oxford, Wallingford, Henley-on-Thames, Windsor, Weybridge and Thames Ditton, before finally entering the City of London.

Some of the facilities here are reasonably basic, but there is electricity, hot showers and a toilet block. A pub and restaurant are within a few minutes' walk. The campsite is just five miles from Oxford, and not far from the A34 and M4.

## site info

**OPEN** April to October

**DIRECTIONS** Five miles south of Oxford, off the A415 Abingdon Road. Turn off the A415 at Clifton Hampden onto High Street. Take the next left and follow the road over the river bridge, leading into the campsite.

**YEP** Showers, toilets, tents, caravans, motorhomes, electric

**NO** Children, dogs, shop, bar, restaurant, play area, equipment hire

**ACTIVITIES** Canoe, kayak, fish

**RATING** Facilities ★★★★★ Location ★★★★★ Water activities ★★★★★

01865 407725

No website

# Benson Waterfront Riverside Park 18
## Benson, Oxfordshire OX10 6SJ

**The posh end of marina camping is at the foot of the Chiltern Hills. Benson Waterfront Riverside Park is a thriving water hole, on the River Thames, within walking distance of the commuter village from which it takes its name. This small campsite exudes the sweet smell of money, in the nicest possible way. The university town of Oxford, with its river walks and historic buildings is a 15-minute drive away.**

Boats, canoes, anglers and wild swimmers are catered for. Benson marina takes care of the moorings, storage, boat repairs and provides Calor gas and diesel. Boat hire is available for short holidays and there are electric craft for hourly or daily hire. A footpath passes through the site leading to quieter areas away from the marina. Anglers need to buy fishing permits. Barbel, bream, chub, pike and roach are all caught. Launching craft is no problem and there's a large ramp available to campers free of charge. Sailing from the site is possible, although as with many river locations, unfavourable winds can be a problem. Avoid heading south (left along the river) as Benson Lock is within a few hundred metres. Its history dates back to the late 1300s, when a mill and weir were recorded.

The views from the front of the campsite are special but some of the pitches are a bit tight. Full touring and camping facilities include en-suite showers and a free laundry service. The adjoining restaurant and bar look right over the river, and on a sunny day, it's a joy to sit on the decked area, watching the world pass by on the river.

## site info

**OPEN** April to October

**DIRECTIONS** Just off the A4074 Oxford to Reading road, opposite the B4009.

**YEP** Dogs, showers, toilets, tents, caravans, motorhomes, electric, shop, bar, restaurant, equipment hire

**NO** Play area

**ACTIVITIES** Canoe, kayak, fish, swim, sailing dinghy

**RATING** Facilities ★★★★★ Location ★★★★★ Water activities ★★★★★

01491 838304

www.bensonwaterfront.co.uk

# south-west england

**The south west oozes good looks, campervans, trendy bars, art festivals and some of the best seafood cuisine in the world. But don't panic if that's not for you: there's plenty of alternative calm around the camping circuit, too. The 250-million-year-old Jurassic Coast – which runs 100 miles from Exmouth in Devon to Studland in Dorset – pulls in the historians, geologists and part-time enthusiasts, and Stonehenge, in Wiltshire, is still popular among the new-age travellers.**

The latest craze is 'coasteering', a sport that involves wearing a crash-helmet while climbing, swimming, abseiling and diving between sea and land (see page 32 for more on coasteering). With the thrills, come the spills. The South West's RNLI is the busiest in the country and beach-related lifeboat launches. Free safety guides are available by emailing beachsafety@rnli.org.uk.

The geography of this region revolves around two national parks – Exmoor and Dartmoor. Exmoor spans Somerset and North Devon. Its rocky cliffs are separated from Wales by the Bristol Channel. The beaches between Combe Martin and Lynmouth are wonderful. The park has three major rivers: the Barle, Exe and Lyn, and two large lakes: Wimbleball and Wistlandpound; all of these spots are excellent for canoeing. Dartmoor, in southern Devon, is further inland. Spread across 368 square miles, its gorse, bogs and grass-covered granite hills can be navigated along the River Dart, which has some of the best canoeing in the county. Devon hosts more than 250 miles of coastline and good diving, with offshore wrecks and reefs to the north and south.

Some of the best sea-fishing is around Appledore and Brixham. The Exe and Tamar are popular rivers for fly-fishing. West of Devon is Dorset and the sandy resorts of Bournemouth and Poole, which are more cosmopolitan than cool, but well worth a look. Europe's first artificial surf reef has been created at Boscombe, a suburb of Bournemouth. Dorset has world-class sailing at Weymouth and Portland, and beaches for mackerel or bass fishing. The sheltered waters of Christchurch Harbour are somewhere to park up and launch a canoe or kayak.

Somerset includes Weston-super-Mare, Burnham-on-Sea, Brean Sands, and harbours, villages and marinas. The Kennet and Avon Canal runs from Bath in the west to Bedwyn in the east. Cornwall is a mecca for sailing, surfing, course fishing and seafood. With 300 beaches, hidden coves, lakes and rivers, Cornwall's aqua-sport credentials rival even the Welsh.

The camping scene is a big part of the surfing community and almost a way of life in this part of the country. For those not keen to park up in council car parks (sometimes illegally), there's plenty of choice. I've stayed at, and documented, almost 100 campsites next to beaches, rivers and lakes, particularly along the dunes of the north coast or around the Cornish inland waters such as Stithians, in Redruth, Siblyback, at Liskeard, and the Tamar Lakes, in Bude.

There's surfing, fishing, wakeboarding, kayaking, windsurfing, rafting, scuba diving, swimming, snorkelling and kitesurfing. It's the ride of a lifetime whatever your age.

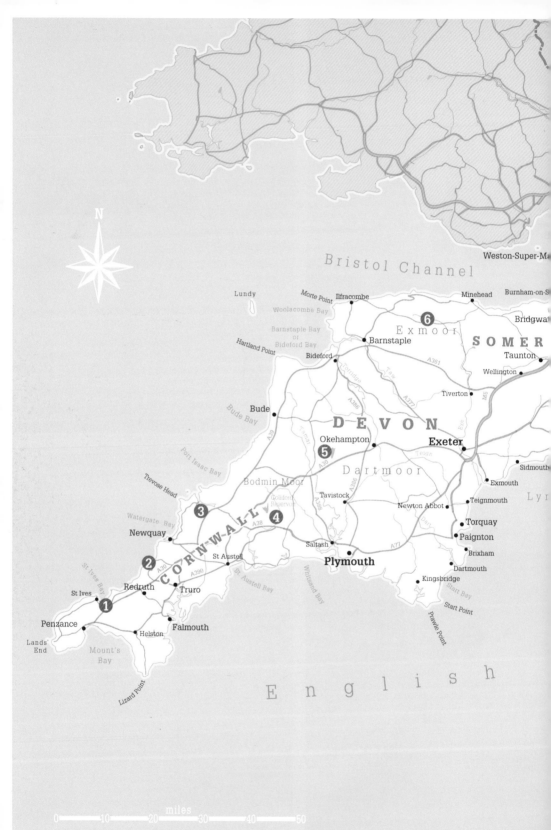

# Sandy Acres ❶
## Hayle, Cornwall TR27 5BA

**Campers arrive here to surf the sea and dunes in this classic landscape. 'Towan' is Cornish for sand dune and 'The Towans' refers to the three-mile stretch of towering sands and grasses that extend north-east from the River Hayle estuary to Gwithian beach. Individual dunes have their own names, such as Hayle Towans, Riviere Towans, Mexico Towans and Gwithian Towans. Some climb 60 metres above sea level.**

Waves can get up to two metres, although Hayle Beach is not the hairiest of the Cornish surfing spots because of the river estuary. It is a good place to learn and there are several surf schools along the beach. Group or individual lessons are available throughout the summer, for all ages. St Ives, on the other side of the estuary to the Towans, is more popular with expert surfers. Wetsuits are a good idea, even if you're only swimming – the Cornish surf schools tend to talk up the effects of the Gulf Stream and the 'natural heat retaining properties' of the bay. Fishing is popular around the mouth of the estuary. An hour before high tide with lugworm, ragworm or peeler crab is best. Lures don't seem to work too well, other than from a canoe or kayak. It's too difficult to get a sailing dinghy over the dunes from the campsite, although there are launch areas within a short drive.

Pitches are spread about a grassy plateau in the dunes. There is no electrical supply, but there are hot showers and a washing-up area, and fresh drinking water is provided. Much of the area from Gwithian to Mexico Towans is protected and designated as a Site of Special Scientific Interest. The South West Coast Path passes through here, offering 630 miles of superb coastal walking via Minehead on the edge of the Exmoor National Park all the way to Poole Harbour in Dorset. A small public car park below the campsite, just before the beach, is used mostly by surfers. Beachside Holiday Park (01736 753080) is worth checking out, 400 metres further along the water's edge. It provides camping in the dunes, too, but with all the facilities you would expect of a major holiday park.

BEACH

## site info

**OPEN** April to October

**DIRECTIONS** Driving away from Hale on the A30, turn left at the roundabout opposite McDonalds, north of Copperhouse. Take the first right onto the B3301 towards Gwithian. Turn left within 300 metres, into Sandy Acres, and follow the track all the way.

**YEP** Dogs, showers, toilets, tents, caravans, motorhomes

**NO** Electric, shop, bar, restaurant, play area, equipment hire

**ACTIVITIES** Canoe, kayak, fish, swim, snorkel, surf

**RATING** Facilities ★★★★★ Location ★★★★★ Water activities ★★★★★

07768 320505

www.sandy-acres.co.uk

# Perran Sands Holiday Park ②
## Perran Sands, Perranporth, Cornwall TR60AQ

**Large holiday parks are not usually my favourites, but this is up there with the best: clean, spacious and with direct access to the dunes. Hike over the top and some of Cornwall's most famous surfing beaches are just waiting to be explored.**

Access to the waves is via a criss-cross of steep, winding paths. Outward across the sands is always a pleasure. The walk home can be a long one – especially after a day's excitement. A surfing school operates on Perranporth beaches throughout the summer. Despite its beauty, this coastline is renowned for currents, so make use of the lifeguard beach and observe the warning flags. Lifeguards patrol from 10 am until 6 pm from May 16 until September 26. Inflatables are not a good idea, but kayaking and fishing are generally fine. Bass are plentiful, either from the shore or the rocks at the end of the beach. They tend to bite better around a southwesterly/westerly swell.

Pitches are spread across a vast grass section. Many of the 363 spaces are supplied with both water and electric. Sand bases make for excellent drainage during rain. Dog walkers have access to 'dune areas'. Facilities include a supermarket (with bakery and off licence), showers, launderette, heated indoor/outdoor pool and fun flume, and internet in the café-bar and on the terrace. Some charges apply. The shops, pubs and clubs are a long walk away from the camp, which might be either good or bad news, depending on what you like. Newquay, St Ives, Carbis Bay and Padstow are all within a short drive.

## site info

**OPEN** April to October

**DIRECTIONS** Leave the A3075 at Goodhavern and take the B3285 towards Perranporth. The site is on the right within less than a mile.

**YEP** Dogs, showers, toilets, tents, caravans, motorhomes, electric, shop, bar, restaurant, play area, equipment hire

**NO** -

**ACTIVITIES** Canoe, kayak, fish, swim, snorkel, sailing dinghy, surf

**RATING** Facilities ★★★★★ Location ★★★★★ Water activities ★★★★★

0871 231 0871 (calls cost 10p per minute plus network extras)

www.haven.com/PerranSands

# Trevitha Farm ③

St Issey, Wadebridge, Cornwall PL27 7QH

**Little Petherick Creek is as peaceful as a deserted school library during half term. Other than birdsong and the occasional canoe gliding past, there's barely a sound.**

Cornwall's sandy beaches are a 10-minute drive, but I'll doubt you'll ever want to leave this little piece of heaven. Rolling pastures lead down to an old stone wall and a slate beach, where the Camel Trail guides walkers to Padstow harbour in 45 minutes. It's much more fun to sail or paddle and it will take about 15 minutes. Most campers bring their own boats and kayaks. Anything larger than a small dinghy can be a problem to launch, as there isn't much room to navigate the boundary wall between beach and campsite. Fishing is wonderful, either from the land or by boat. Mullet, bass and flounder can be caught. The creek is tidal and flows into the Camel Estuary, which stretches from Wadebridge downstream to the open sea at Padstow Bay. Swimming here is wonderful.

As this is a Caravan Club CL, there are just five pitches spread about the 1.5-acre site. Wildflowers, hedges and the rolling terrain naturally divide off individual areas. There are no toilets or showers. Other than occasional hikers on the Camel Trail below, herons, gulls, egrets, buzzards and badgers are the main visitors. The public footpath runs along the creek (and joins the Saint's Way footpath at Little Petherick). Walking and cycling is also good towards Wadebridge or Bodmin. Two pubs, the Pickwick Inn and the Ring o' Bells, are within easy reach. St Issey village is just over a mile away.

**BEST IN Cornwall**

## site info

**OPEN** March to October (and winter subject to ground and weather conditions)

**DIRECTIONS** West of Wadebridge, turn right off the A389 in St Issey, at the Ring o' Bells pub. Continue and bear left at Pickwick Inn. After about a mile, pass farm buildings. Campsite is behind a gate a few hundred yards on.

**YEP** Dogs, caravans, motorhomes, electric

**NO** Showers, toilets, shop, bar, tents, restaurant, play area, equipment hire

**ACTIVITIES** Canoe, kayak, fish, swim, snorkel, sailing dinghy

**RATING** Facilities ★★☆☆☆ Location ★★★★★ Water activities ★★★★★

01841 540574

No website

# Siblyback Lake Country Park Campsite ④
## Common Moor, Liskeard, Cornwall PL14 6ER

**Fly-fishermen hook rainbow trout up to eight pounds in size from boat or shore at Siblyback Lake, next to Bodmin Moor. Angling, sailing and windsurfing courses are all available. Campers bring their own craft or hire. All boats need third-party insurance and should be no longer than 18-feet (no powered craft).**

Seven angling boats are available to hire, including a 'wheelyboat' for disabled anglers. The fishing season opens in March and ends on October 31. Equipment can be bought or hired on-site, as can day and season tickets. Tutors provide flyfishing tuition. Beginners and family fishing days are held in partnership with the Environment Agency. RYA sailing and windsurfing courses are put on throughout the year. Cable wakeboarding, kneeboarding and water-skiing were introduced in 2012. A 40ft 'High Rope' course in the tree tops is for families who like an on-land challenge.

There's just a handful of pitches, which means the camp has a relaxed feel about it. Local scout groups sometimes use the extra field next door. Facilities include showers, washing-up facilities, waste disposal and a café. A cycle path was recently created around the lake. Nearby Liskeard hosts one of Cornwall's last remaining livestock markets.

## site info

**OPEN** March to October

**DIRECTIONS** Take the Bolventor junction off the A30 and follow the brown signs. From the A38, follow the signs from Twelvewoods roundabout at Dobwalls.

**YEP** Dogs, showers, toilets, tents, caravans, motorhomes, electric, shop, café, equipment hire

**NO** Bar

**ACTIVITIES** Canoe, kayak, fish, sailing dinghy

**RATING** Facilities ★★★★★ Location ★★★★★ Water activities ★★★★★

01579 346522

www.swlakestrust.org.uk/leisure-activities/camping/siblyback-lake

# Northam Farm Caravan & Touring Park
South Road, Brean, Burnham-on-Sea, Somerset TA8 2SE 6

**Northam Farm is on South Road at the centre of a parade of funfairs, amusements and activities. Between Burnham-on-Sea and Weston-super-Mare, it's perfect for families who like to fish and holiday.**

Despite such a central location, the park is relatively quiet and the lake is mostly tranquil. Bait and rods are sold at the on-site shop. Forty-two pegs are spaced around the water's edge. Bream, carp, chub, perch, roach and tench are common. Fishing is allowed from an hour before sunrise until an hour after sunset. Swimming is not allowed. Sea-fishing for conger, bass and flounder is very good at Burnham or Weston, where it's also possible to charter boats.

Excellent facilities are provided by the owners – the same family that has run the park for more than 65 years. A playground, BMX track and football pitch keep kids entertained. The shop stocks all the basics and there's a launderette. Showers and toilets are excellent (although there's a small charge for hot water). Campers without dogs get access to a pooch-free field. The Seagull Inn and Scotty's Bar offer decent food and drink that isn't too expensive. There is an on-site service centre for caravans and motorhomes, payable at an hourly rate.

## site info

**OPEN** April to October

**DIRECTIONS** Leave the M5 at Junction 22, following the signs to Burnham-on-Sea / Brean. Northam Farm is just after Brean village on the right, half a mile past Brean Leisure Park.

**YEP** Dogs, showers, toilets, tents, caravans, motorhomes, electric, shop, bar, restaurant, play area,

**NO** Equipment hire

**ACTIVITIES** Fish

**RATING** Facilities ★★★★★ Location ★★★★★ Water activities ★★★★★

01278 751244

www.northamfarm.com

# Channel View

Brean, Somerset TA8 2RR

**At this site you have a rare chance to savour sea water and salt air, but the fun really starts when the tide goes out. Channel View sits between Weston and Burnham-on-Sea overlooking the impressive headland at the mouth of the River Severn. Brean is a tiny resort, renowned for miles of golden sand, holiday centres and land-yacht sailing.**

The surfing is better here than at Weston. The waves are bigger and there's usually less wind, thanks to the landscape. Two hours either side of high tide is best for sailing. Those with the largest craft must launch from nearby Berrow Beach. Brean Land Yacht Club has its origins in the early part of the 20th century, when the locals began sailing with yachts made from the remains of First World War aircraft. People who sail these craft are still called 'pilots' and they can reach speeds of up 60 miles per hour. The club holds regular trial days for newbies. Windsurfing here is fun, too. Fishing from the beach is best a few hours before the flood tide, when codling come in to feed. Skate, flounder and whiting are also common. Be wary of the fast incoming water. When the water is rough, you'll need waders to get out into the shallows and cast beyond the surf. Frozen mackerel and squid work well for bait. Try ragworm if fishing for conger. Kayak fishing is excellent.

Channel View is the only touring park with direct access to Brean Sands. Toilets and shower blocks are clean, but can get busy in the high season. Wardens are very apologetic and helpful, but really an upgrade was due when we visited. Washing-up areas and chemical disposal points are available. There's a convenience store, launderette, café, bar and restaurant within walking distance. Dogs can be exercised on the beach, no problem.

## site info

**OPEN** April to October

**DIRECTIONS** Drive north out of Burnham-on-Sea on the coast road. The campsite cannot be missed, 5 miles on the left.

**YEP** Dogs, showers, toilets, tents, caravans, motorhomes, electric

**NO** Shop, bar, restaurant, play area, equipment hire

**ACTIVITIES** Canoe, kayak, fish, swim, snorkel, sailing dinghy, surf

**RATING** Facilities ★★★★★ Location ★★★★★ Water activities ★★★★★

01278 751055

www.breanfarm.co.uk/channel-view.html

# Uphill Boat Services 🔟

## Uphill Wharf, Weston-super-Mare, Somerset BS23 4XR

**We were lost, looking for a particular campsite that someone had recommended. After asking for directions at Uphill Wharf, we were told the site we wanted had closed. That was the bad news. The good news was that the wharf owner had created his own touring field, right on the Bristol Channel, within a five-minute walk of Weston-super-Mare beach, and this is it.**

Boats of all sizes can be launched here. Both the owner and the members at the adjoining boat club offer good advice. Weston Bay Yacht Club has a programme of racing, cruising and social events. Access to the Bristol Channel is via the tidal river. Tides can be exceptionally high and some parts of the campsite area are prone to taking on water. A lake has been created to cope with the wash and it makes a great place for kids to fish or boat, especially as fish get trapped in the lake during high tides. Launching canoes and kayaks is easy, and once out onto the sea, the tidal currents are relatively safe to navigate. Waves aren't always great for surfing, although the waters are popular among windsurfers and kitesurfers. Fishing is best on the beach an hour either side of high tide. Cast 30 metres out using lug or ragworm for flounders, bass and conger.

Twenty-one pitches are spread around the riverbank, lake and nature reserve. Electric hook-ups are available on hard-standing pitches, and the owner has plans to install more. Showers and toilets are OK. Buy drinks and snacks from the chandlery store. A tearoom provides breakfasts, lunches and cream teas. For walkers, the Mendip Trail starts here and there are climbing activities on the cliffs overhead. A local bus services stops right outside the wharf entrance for Weston Town and Pier. Brean Down peninsular is a short drive.

## site info

**OPEN** All year

**DIRECTIONS** Approach Weston-super-Mare from the south on the A370. At the Weston Hospital roundabout, take the first exit left into Grange Road. Turn right at the mini-roundabout and then left into Uphill Way. Follow the road for half a mile and then turn left into Uphill Wharf.

**YEP** Dogs, showers, toilets, tents, caravans, motorhomes, electric, shop, restaurant

**NO** Bar, play area, equipment hire

**ACTIVITIES** Canoe, kayak, fish, swim, sailing dinghy

**RATING** Facilities ★★★★★ Location ★★★★★ Water activities ★★★★★

01934 418617

www.uphillboatservices.co.uk

BEST IN Somerset

# Bath Marina & Caravan Park ⑪
## Brassmill Lane, Bath, Somerset BA1 3JT

**Bath is famous for its theatres, baths, arts and parks. Bath Marina, just two miles away on the green banks of the River Avon, is like a peaceful base camp for anyone intent on scaling the city's high art.**

The Avon is navigable to the Severn Estuary. Canoes and kayaks are easy to launch from the side of the river. Access is unrestricted as far as Reading and the River Thames upstream, via the Kennet and Avon Canal. Fishing isn't allowed on this section, so cyclists and walkers make good use of the towpath alongside the site. Bacon's Tackle Shop, on the Lower Bristol Road, Bath, provides permits and advice on where and how to fish the river.

Pitches are surrounded by trees with 64 hard-standing bases. Hard-standing pitches have concrete bases, which mean a little time and patience is needed to find some softer ground to pitch awnings. Groceries are available on-site and there's a bakery delivery service. A bus service runs into Bath every 15 minutes from outside the campsite. Pubs are within easy walking distance, along the riverbank in either direction. Bath Music Festival is one of the highlights of the year, in May and June. Bristol International Balloon Fiesta in August attracts 500,000 people.

## site info

**OPEN** All year

**DIRECTIONS** Follow the A4 into Bath. Cross the River Avon bridge on the Newbridge Road/A4 and take the first right onto Brassmill Lane and then first right into the campsite.

**YEP** Dogs, showers, equipment hire, toilets, caravans, motorhomes, electric, shop

**NO** Bar, restaurant, play area, tents

**ACTIVITIES** Canoe, kayak

**RATING** Facilities ★★★★★ Location ★★★★★ Water activities ★★★★★

01225 424301

www.bwml.co.uk/marinas/bath_marina_and_caravan_park

# Stowford Manor Farm

Wingfield, Trowbridge, Wiltshire BA14 9LH

**We call it the Foam 'n' Frome because of the bubbles on the river next to the Mill. Stowford Manor Farm is a family-run campsite on the grounds of a former medieval settlement.**

The Somerset River Frome rises near Witham Friary and joins the River Avon south of Bath (it is not to be confused with the Frome in Dorset). Farleigh and District Swimming Club is 200 metres away and claims to be the only river swimming club in the country. Founded in 1933, the club has more than 2,000 members who swim in a clear, deep part of the river above a weir. Family membership is good value, and provides access to toilets, changing rooms and a large car park. If you're on a tight budget, younger kids can have plenty of fun taking a dip in the shallows back at the campsite and chasing the ducks. Makeshift swing tyres hang from the trees.

Facilities include electric hook-up, toilets, a recently renovated stable block with showers, sinks and washing-up area with free hot water. A lovely tearoom on-site has a classic English feel about it. Cream teas are served up with the farm's own Jersey cream and homemade scones. Bed and breakfast is available in the Mill House, also with some ingredients sourced from the farm. Art-and-crafts workshops are held at the manor – full details are featured on the website. There's a walk along the river to Farleigh Castle. Campers can also cycle on the nearby Kennet and Avon Canal or take a short drive to Bradford-on-Avon, Bath and Longleat Safari Park.

BEST IN
Wiltshire

## site info

**OPEN** April to October

**DIRECTIONS** Two miles west of Trowbridge on the A366. Signposted on the left, ¼ mile before Farleigh Hungerford.

**YEP** Dogs, showers, toilets, tents, caravans, motorhomes, restaurant, electric

**NO** Shop, bar, play area, equipment hire

**ACTIVITIES** fish, swim

**RATING** Facilities ★★★★★ Location ★★★★★ Water activities ★★★★★

01225 752253

www.stowfordmanorfarm.co.uk

# Seadown Caravan Park ⑬
Bridge Road, Charmouth, Dorset DT6 6QS

**Seadown is squeezed between river and sea, beside the River Char and with direct access to Charmouth beach. Fossil walks are organised by the Heritage Centre, which then displays any rare exhibits that are found.**

The river hugs the eastern edge of the caravan park. Fishing is possible on the river, although it is better on the beach. Sand eel and squid make bait for bass and rays. Kayaking offshore is fun, but check the tides. Surf an hour after high tide, particularly when close to the mouth of the river. Boats can't be launched directly from the site, so drive onto the sand from the shingle beach car park nearby, where a car park attendant collects the launch fee. There is also a day charge for storing boats on the campsite.

Facilities include showers, washing-up sinks, toilets, hairdryers, a launderette and a shop. Tennis, badminton, skittles or table tennis can be played on-site. Charmouth is a short walk and the seaside town of Lyme Regis is about three miles west.

## site info

**OPEN** March to October

**DIRECTIONS** From the east, leave the A35 Bridport to Charmouth road signposted to Charmouth. Continue down the hill and past the caravan sales on the left-hand side. Drive over the bridge and turn left into Bridge Road at the Seadown sign. Campsite is straight ahead after a few hundred metres.

**YEP** Dogs, showers, toilets, tents, caravans, motorhomes, electric, shop, play area

**NO** Bar, restaurant, equipment hire

**ACTIVITIES** Canoe, kayak, fish, swim, surf

**RATING** Facilities ★★★★★ Location ★★★★★ Water activities ★★★★★

01297 560154

www.seadownholidaypark.co.uk

# Meadowbank Holidays 14

Stour Way, Christchurch, Dorset BH23 2PQ

**The Stour is reputed to be one of the best river fisheries in the UK. For those not into angling, Meadowbank offers a tranquil setting a few miles from beaches of Bournemouth, the Dorset Jurassic Coast and the New Forest.**

Fish regularly include 15-pound barbel and 8-pound chub, as well as roach, perch, dace, large pike and the odd carp. During the summer, mullet swim upstream from Christchurch and can occasionally be caught around the campsite. Float fishing with hemp and tares is good for roach. Bread flakes or cheese paste work for chub. Maggots and casters are better for barbel, although the smaller silver fish can become a problem. Permits can be bought for the camping side of the river. Day permits for the Throop fishery, which includes both sides of the river, are available from local tackle shops.

The Stour can accommodate canoes or swimmers, although there may be problems along the way with the fisheries manager or the water keeper and fishermen. The estate owning the river claims permissions are needed if paddling either side from the campsite. No permission is needed between Iford Bridge and Christchurch Harbour, as the river here is tidal. Sea and estuary fishing at Christchurch harbour is excellent. The Quay is one of the best mullet venues in the country. Anglers have good success fishing with bread from mid-June.

Conifers and hanging baskets contribute to the park-like setting. There are three types of touring pitches. Fully serviced pitches are on a tarmac base, with pea shingle for awnings, equipped with individual drinking water and waste points; larger pitches are on grass; standard non-awning plots are for small campervans and two-berth caravans. Hot showers are excellent and free. There is a dishwashing area, launderette, baby-change facilities and baths. Gas is available and the park has a shop supplying basic food and camping gear. There is a games room, pool table and children's play area.

## site info

**OPEN** March to October

**DIRECTIONS** Pass Ringwood and take the A338 towards Bournemouth. After 5 miles take the first exit left, towards Christchurch on the B3073 and follow directions to the park.

**YEP** showers, toilets, caravans, motorhomes, electric, shop, play area,

**NO** Dogs, tents, bar, restaurant, equipment hire

**ACTIVITIES** Fish, canoe (check permission)

**RATING** Facilities ★★★★★ Location ★★★★★ Water activities ★★★★★

01202 483597

www.meadowbank-holidays.co.uk

**BEST IN**
Dorset

# south-east england

This is the place I call home; it's where my heart is. I'm not embarrassed to say my dad has a lot to do with that. He's been called an 'Essex beach bum' ever since his family moved to Southend from the East End, almost 60 years ago. He aspired to swim in the Thames Estuary almost every spare moment he had outside of work. Up at 5.30 am, hoping to finish at 2 pm and then driving his van down to the beaches at Chalkwell or Westcliff-on-Sea. As a family, we were there most weekends during the long summers of 1966 to 1980. Now in his mid-70s, he still swims from April to October at high tide, a few metres from the sea wall. At low tide he strides out in his emerald green Speedos across the mudflats to the creeks where he keeps company with terns, seals, grey mullet – and the past. He calls it the most peaceful place in the world.

Peace is at a premium around here. The UK has the worst congestion in Europe. The south east is the most populated, congested region in England and Essex's roads are the most overused of all. Heading for the hills isn't an option – there are no rocky peaks or lakeland escapes. What we do have are estuaries, rivers, coastal villages, town resorts and a multitude of creeks and inlets. Behind the shoreline is patchwork of run-down estates, village halls and opulence segregated by green belt, parks and inequalities in education. But for all their problems, the people from the home counties share a collective passion: the outdoors.

The New Forest stretches across 140,000 acres of ancient woodland and wild grassland. Although not renowned for waterscapes, its borders brim with water. The Solent has 23,000 moorings, nearby Fordingbridge sits on the banks of the River Avon, Lymington is celebrated for its sailing history, and Hayling Island and the Isle of Wight are as close to new-age holiday resorts as I've found. Move along to West and East Sussex and villages are huddled around tidal inlets (Bosham, near Chichester harbour) chalk cliffs and sandy peninsulas. Even the beautiful seaside towns (Bexhill, Shoreham-by-Sea) are being rediscovered by Britain's new wave of budget-conscious tourists. Essex's beauty stretches from Brightlingsea and Mersea Island in the north, to the industrial Thames regions of Canvey and Thurrock. Leigh-on-Sea is among the most attractive towns on the Thames estuary, with its cobbled streets, pubs and cottages. A small community of transient wild campers park all year round on Leigh's Two Tree Island car park, next to a public launch ramp into the tidal creeks. These shallow waters offer access to Kent, London and to Essex's 350 miles of coastline – the longest of any English county. The trail inland boasts wealth and water, too: great fishing, boating and swimming.

For all of its coastal appeal, fisheries and small lakes dominate the camping scene in the South East. Carp angling and camping is big business. Rivers are popular for those who prefer silver fish, pike and the wild challenge..

..The sun shines more here than in other parts of the country. The region enjoys the highest temperatures and the least amount of rain. If the scenery is less spectacular, the upside is the opportunity to peel off waterproofs and wetsuits, and savour some solar.

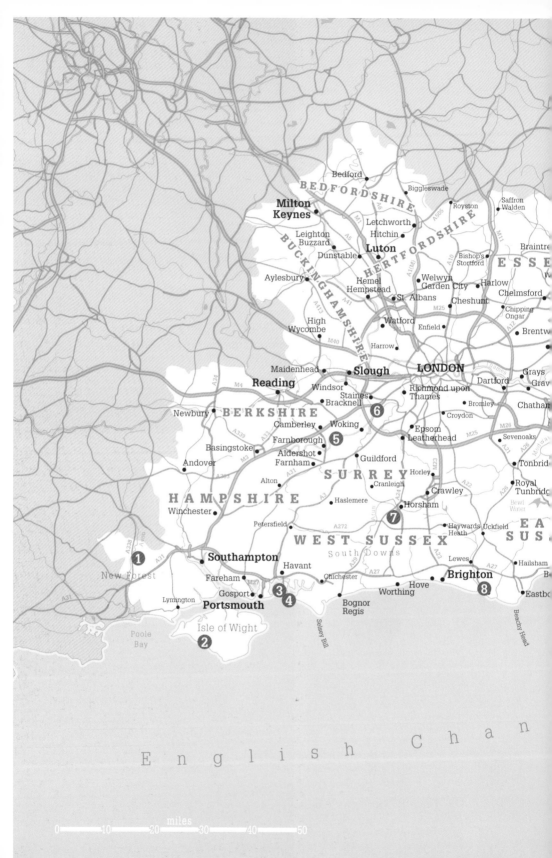

# New Forest Water Park ❶

Ringwood Road, Fordingbridge, Hampshire SP6 2EY

**Watersports are the daytime entertainment; campfires and barbecues provide the fun by night. This a family-run business set in 50 acres on the edge of the New Forest. Christchurch, Bournemouth and Southampton are nearby.**

Whether you're taking part or just watching, the lake is the main focus. Waterskiing, wakeboarding and water-rides keep adults and kids aged six and upwards entertained. Kayaks and paddle boards (bit like a surf board with a long-handled single oar) can be hired, along with wetsuits and tuition. Anglers who want to fish are allowed to stay on a private island in the centre of the lake for two or five nights. Carp weighing more than 42 pounds have been caught and some catfish weigh up to 55 pounds. Fishing around the rest of the water is, sadly, for club members only.

Several pitches are spread about the one-acre field next to the water. A few more pitches are set back in the adjoining woodland. Logs are sold at reception for campfires, which are a nice touch on warm and cool evenings. Showers and a single loo, one each for men and women, are open from 9 am until 8 pm. They can get pretty busy during the summer months. An overnight portable loo is available for campers, but bring your own paper just in case. Bearing in mind the limited facilities and lack of power, pitches are not cheap, and there's no electrical supply. Staff are very friendly and the bar is an excellent meeting place, with views over the lake. Small supermarkets are two miles away in Fordingbridge or go four miles to Ringwood for more.

## site info

**OPEN** April to September

**DIRECTIONS** From Ringwood take the A338 signposted Fordingbridge and Salisbury. After 3 miles, pass the Old Beams pub on the right. Campsite is 1 mile after this on the left. From Fordingbridge, it is 2 miles on the right. Look out for the brown tourist signs saying New Forest Water Park.

**YEP** Showers, toilets, tents, caravans, motorhomes, equipment hire, bar, restaurant

**NO** Electric, shop, dogs, play area

**ACTIVITIES** Water skis, wakeboarding, kayak, fish (restricted) and rides

**RATING** Facilities ★★★★★ Location ★★★★★ Water activities ★★★★★

01425 656868

www.newforestwaterpark.co.uk

# Grange Farm ②
## Military Road, Brighstone Bay, Isle of Wight PO30 4DA

**Grange Farm is on a surfing beach below a weather-beaten cliff. It is a working ranch populated by alpaca, llama and water buffalo. If it already sounds like a fairy tale, that's not the half of it. There are fossils scattered all over the crumbling rock face and the scenery is dramatic. 'Chine' is the name given to river valleys that flow out to sea. Freshwater and Compton Bay, Blackgang Chine, the Needles and Alum Bay are all nearby, as are the resorts of Ventnor and Shanklin.**

An exposed English Channel makes this one of the best beaches on the south coast for surfing. Take care of the rocks at low tide. Reef breaks are also good further along the coast between the Chines. The beach fishes at high tide, but the weed can be annoying. Surfers and anglers sometimes clash. Spinning or lures from kayaks are a better option. Codling, pollock, rays and bass are common. Plenty of campers swim here. The steep track means it's not possible to launch a sailing dinghy.

There are 60 pitches scattered about the field. Electric hook-ups and water points are spread about. Those with tents should bring plenty of pegs and strong canvas, as the site is exposed to the winds that take care of whipping up the surf. Toilets and showers are plentiful and clean. Expect a small charge for washing machines and tumble dryer. Facilities include a children's playground and a shop that stocks basics and camping essentials. The whole area is good for cycling and walking. Paleontologists are usually around to identify whatever prehistoric remains they've dug up. In the village are pubs, tearooms, a National Trust shop and a museum. Brighstone Holiday Centre is an OK alternative if Grange Farm is closed.

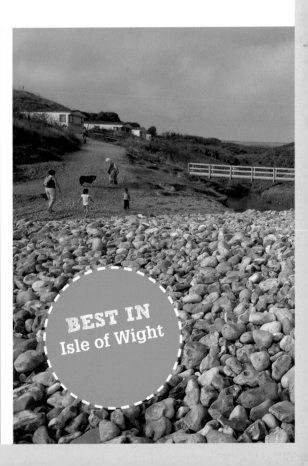

## site info

**OPEN** March to November

**DIRECTIONS** From Fishbourne or Cowes head towards Newport. At Carisbrooke take the A3323 road to Brighstone. Just before the village take a left turning by the church, into New Road.

**YEP** Dogs, showers, toilets, tents, caravans, motorhomes, electric, shop, play area

**NO** Bar, restaurant, equipment hire

**ACTIVITIES** Canoe, kayak, fish, swim, surf

**RATING** Facilities ★★★★★ Location ★★★★★ Water activities ★★★★★

01983 740296

www.grangefarmholidays.com

BEST IN
Isle of Wight

# Fleet Farm Camping & Caravan Site ③

Yew Tree Road, Hayling Island, Hampshire PO11 0QE

**Small islands tend to retain something of a bygone feel about them and Hayling Island is no exception. I'm not saying it is the place that time forgot, but it certainly smacks of yesteryear. Personally, I love it.**

Windsurfers, small boats and kayaks can be launched directly from the site, with access to the fantastic waterscape of Chichester Harbour. The entire area of water is bordered by a system of intricate creeks brimming with wildlife, most of which is only navigable by canoe or kayak. Langstone Harbour, on the western side of Hayling, can be reached by sailing either way around the island. Kids enjoy catching crabs, swimming, fishing and netting tiddlers at low tide. A new warden started in June 2011 – he was friendly, had his own his own yacht and was knowledgeable about the tides, fishing and boating in the area. More than a year on, he'd lost none of his enthusiasm.

Old oak trees surround the 75 pitches on either side, and to the front is the tidal creek. I'd read and heard complaints about the loos and showers. The racing green barn-style toilet doors look like they've come out of a defunct secondary modern school that was demolished in the 1970s and the matching showers have less style than a geriatric underwear convention, but the water is always hot and the cubicles are mostly clean. There is a play area. The beach is OK, but stony. The sands, seafront and Hayling Seaside Railway are only a few minutes away by car, with easy parking all year. A pub is within walking distance and West Quay Shopping Centre is handy, too.

## site info

**OPEN** March to November

**DIRECTIONS** Follow the A3023 over the road bridge on to the Island. After 2 miles turn left in to Copse Lane, opposite Stoke fruit farm. The site is signposted on the right.

**YEP** Dogs, showers, toilets, tents, caravans, motorhomes, electric

**NO** Shop, bar, restaurant, equipment hire

**ACTIVITIES** Canoe, kayak, fish, swim, sailing dinghy

**RATING** Facilities ★★★★★ Location ★★★★★ Water activities ★★★★★

02392 463684

www.haylingcampsites.co.uk

# Fishery Creek Caravan & Camping Park

## 100 Fishery Lane, Hayling Island, Hampshire PO11 9NR

**A waterside phenomenon between a tidal creek and a lake on Hampshire's 'Sunshine Island'. The sea access to the ria (coastal inlet) of Chichester Harbour is remarkable. Portsmouth, Bournemouth, The New Forest and South Downs are a short drive away.**

Fishery Creek's northern edge overlooks a lake and fountain. More exciting, though, is the private slipway on the east shore, with access to the sea. It's a natural harbour, almost two miles wide, formed by the gap between the mainland of West Sussex and the upside down 'T' shape of Hayling Island. These sheltered waters provide perfect conditions for sailing, windsurfing, kitesurfing and canoeing. An Act of Parliament protects their status as one of south England's last undeveloped coastal regions. The Chichester Harbour Conservancy Act of 1971 has a duty to conserve, maintain and improve the harbour for recreation, natural conservation and natural beauty. Fishing from the beach, boat or kayak is excellent. Multiple feathers and hooks work well. Swimming is good here, too, although powerboats and jet skis are launched from the campsite, so take care. It's common to see queues of visitors, with trailers, trying to get onto the site on a summer weekend. The Ferry Boat Inn has a notice board inside the main door listing information and phone numbers for hiring boats. Bream, plaice and mackerel can be fished out of the creek beside camp.

All pitches are on grass, although some have chipped-bark areas for awnings. Quite a few are seasonals, but the best pitches creek-side are set aside for holidaying tourers and caravans. Some are separated by post and chain fencing. Showers and toilets are modern and clean. A five-minute stroll along the creek will take you to the beach, local shops, restaurants, pubs and clubs.

## site info

**OPEN** March to October

**DIRECTIONS** Once you get onto Hayling Island, follow the A3023 down towards the seafront. Turn right at the bottom and then follow the signs for campsite

**YEP** Dogs, showers, toilets, tents, caravans, motorhomes, electric, shop, play area

**NO** Bar, restaurant, equipment hire

**ACTIVITIES** Canoe, kayak, fish, swim, sailing dinghy

**RATING** Facilities ★★★★★ Location ★★★★★ Water activities ★★★★★

02392 462164

www.fisherycreekpark.co.uk

BEST IN Hampshire

# Basingstoke Canal Centre ⑤

Mytchett Place Road, Mytchett, Surrey GU16 6DD

**Everything seems to stand still in the village of Mytchett; people, time, boats – even the water. The Canal Centre is a brief interlude along a 32-mile-long towpath where visitors and travellers come to relax, reflect and drink coffee. Its towpath stretches from the village of Greywell in Hampshire to Woodham in Surrey. Engineers built the canal between 1788 and 1794 to connect Basingstoke and the River Thames via the Wey Navigation.**

Canoes and boats still navigate the entire length of the canal. It's possible to cruise for a couple of miles in either direction of the campsite before reaching a lock. Basingstoke Canal Angling Association (BCAA) controls fishing rights, and has spent more than £40,000 on stock since 1992. Waters around the centre are probably less fished than some other areas, simply because there are so many people around. Roach and tench are common, and are most likely to bite early morning or late evening. Crayfish can be caught in traps, but only the American Red Signal crayfish and you need to have an Environment Agency license (available online). It is illegal to catch the white-clawed crayfish, which is indigenous to the UK. Advice on how and where to catch crayfish, and on fishing on the canal, is available from the BCAA Fisheries Officer. Unless you're a swan or duck, I'd pass on the swimming. The canal can be very still, and gets a little whiffy on a long hot summer's day.

Pitches are open all year in a large field next to the centre. Toilets and shower facilities are available. Electric isn't provided, but 'quiet' generators (I've never seen one yet) are allowed from 9 am until 8.30 pm. The centre also has a picnic and play area, gift shop, visitors' centre and tearoom.

## site info

**OPEN** All year

**DIRECTIONS** Leave the M3 at junction 4 on the A331 towards Farnham. Turn off for Mytchett and follow signs for the Canal Visitor Centre.

**YEP** Dogs, showers, toilets, tents, caravans, motorhomes, shop, bar, restaurant, play area, equipment hire

**NO** Electric

**ACTIVITIES** Canoe, kayak, fish

**RATING** Facilities ★★★★★ Location ★★★★★ Water activities ★★★★★

01252 370073

www3.hants.gov.uk/Basingstoke-canal/campsite.htm

# Chertsey Camping & Caravanning Club Site ⑥

Bridge Road, Chertsey, Surrey KT16 8JX

**A rural setting less than 30 minutes from the bright lights of London. Chertsey is part of the Surrey commuter belt but when I'm relaxing here, work is the last thing on my mind. Trains carry visitors right into the centre of London with easy access to Big Ben, Windsor Castle, Kew Gardens, theatres, restaurants and shopping.**

Pitches are shadowed by trees, surrounded by bushes and bordered by the River Thames. Canoes and boats launch from along the east side of the site. The park hosts canoe-camping events throughout the year. Campers can fish or swim in the river thanks to a successful clean-up and several campaigns to return the river to its natural, unpolluted state. More than 100 different species of fish have returned, including salmon and sea trout. The Thames was awarded the international Theiss river prize for river management and conservation in 2010. Sailing is possible, although it's only possible to launch dinghies from this site.

Pitches are well spaced out on hard-standing and grass. The best are the grass pitches right next to the river, but they close in winter because of flooding. Showers and toilets are very clean. A TV and games room is popular with youngsters at night. Wi-Fi is available in some parts of the park. Walk along the towpath to Staines using part of the Thames Path National Trail, check out the deer in Richmond Park. Three nearby racecourses include Epsom Downs, Kempton Park and Sandown Park. Thorpe Park is 10 minutes away.

BEST IN
Surrey

## site info

**OPEN** All year

**DIRECTIONS** Just off the B375, west of where the road bridge crosses the River Thames.

**YEP** Dogs, electric, showers, toilets, tents, caravans, motorhomes, play area

**NO** Bar, restaurant, equipment hire

**ACTIVITIES** Canoe, kayak, fish, swim, sailing dinghy

**RATING** Facilities ★★★★★ Location ★★★★★ Water activities ★★★★★

01932 562405

www.campingandcaravanningclub.co.uk/chertsey

# Sumners Ponds ①

Chapel Road, Horsham, West Sussex RH13 0PR

**Fishing from inside a camping pitch is my idea of a perfect holiday: playing at the hunter/gatherer, but in a secluded, peaceful and homely environment. Kindred spirits share the midnight oil. Sumners Ponds is part of a working farm in the West Sussex countryside, 10 minutes from the town of Horsham. What makes it a bit different is the underground spring that helped create the four fishing lakes.**

The fishery is open to the public from 7 am until dusk, although campers and members can start angling from 6 am. Each lake is stocked with carp, pike or easy-to-catch silver fish. Carp have weighed in at 34 pounds and pike up to 15 pounds. A resident water bailiff offers good advice and stocks bait and tackle in the campsite café and shop. It's only possible to fish after dusk by becoming a member of Sumners Ponds.

Most of the 100 pitches come with electric hook-ups. Nine angler's pitches, with dedicated waterside sections (known as swims) for two people to fish, are the best. All pitches are a mixture of hard-standing and grass, and tents are allowed. Showers, toilets, laundry and washing-up areas are clean. As the lake access is very open, the Bluebell Park camping zone is considered more suitable for kids, with a play area next to woods. The visitor centre, reception and licensed café are next to the water and make a great place to sit. Fried breakfasts and other meals are available as takeaway or eat-in. Groceries and basic camping gear are sold in the shop. Wi-Fi is available on the decked seating area next to the lake. Staff are very friendly. Paths and cycle routes surround the campsite. The Queen's Head pub serves good food and beer. Brighton is half an hour away by car.

BEST IN
West Sussex

## site info

**OPEN** All year

**DIRECTIONS** Follow the A264 for Billingshurst and Bognor. Pass the Toyota garage on the right. Turn left immediately after the humpback bridge signed to Barns Green and Christ's Hospital. Follow road for 2 miles. Pass through village, cross small bridge over stream and turn into Sumners Ponds campsite on your right.

**YEP** Dogs, showers, toilets, tents, caravans, motorhomes, electric, shop, bar/restaurant, café, play area

**NO** Equipment hire

**ACTIVITIES** fish

**RATING** Facilities ★★★★★ Location ★★★★★ Water activities ★★★★★

01403 732539

www.sumnersponds.co.uk

# Buckle Holiday Park 8

Marine Parade, Seaford, East Sussex BN25 2QR

**Buckle is like an old sailor: rough round the edges, with loads of character and a tale or two to tell. A ramp leads onto the stony beach for campers wanting to bathe, surf, fish or stroll into town. At low tide, the vast sandy shoreline is exposed.**

Sailing is a good option, as the beach is relatively sheltered from the weather systems either side of the Atlantic and North Sea. The yachting centre next door offers advice on tides and hazards. Fishing from the shore in the summer produces mainly mackerel and garfish caught on spinners and lures. It's not uncommon to see whole shoals of mackerel. If you get bored catching them, try bottom baits for flounders and sole. High tides can be better for codling, gurnard and bass. Dusk and dawn are best, when there are no people swimming. Boat fishing all around is good. Tope and ling can be caught few miles offshore, from a kayak, but great care is needed and you should definitely not go alone. Seaford Bay has been awarded a blue flag for cleanliness. Surfing is OK, as the southwesterly gales create a wind swell that generates decent waves. Birling Gap, east of Seaford, is most popular for more experienced surfers. The southwesterly facing beach, where Beachy Head meets the Seven Sisters, is a beautiful stretch of channel shoreline, and well worth a visit.

More than 100 pitches are laid out on flat grass – mostly spacious and with electrical supply – with an even mix of seasonal and short-term pitches. Seasonals are at the back of the site rather than the front. I was told by one of the caravan owners that this was because the sea wall can be breached by high tides in winter. A separate area is available for tents. Toilet and shower blocks looked like they needed a lick of paint when we visited in 2011. Other facilities include a bar, dishwashing areas, chemical disposal point, freezing of ice packs and laundry room. Gas and camping gas are sold in the office. The park is on the western edge of town, between Brighton and Eastbourne, just off the A259, a short drive from the South Downs. Ferries at Newhaven are less than two miles away and carry day-trippers to Dieppe. The railway station is only a short walk.

BEST IN
East Sussex

# site info

**OPEN** All year (depending on weather)

**DIRECTIONS** Just off the A259, on Marine Parade, at the north-west corner of Seaford.

**YEP** Dogs, showers, toilets, tents, caravans, motorhomes, electric, shop, bar, restaurant

**NO** Play area, equipment hire

**ACTIVITIES** Canoe, kayak, surf, fish, swim, sail

**RATING** Facilities ★★★★★ Location ★★★★★ Water activities ★★★★★

01323 897 801

www.buckleholidaypark.co.uk

# Chequertree Fishery ⑨
## Bethersden, Ashford, Kent TN26 3JR

**Two good reasons to come here: Firstly, you will learn how to fly-fish. Secondly, you will actually catch something. The trout lake is an easy introduction compared to the fast-flowing rivers anglers graduate to once they've caught the bug. Set in the countryside, on the outskirts of Bethersden, Ashford is five miles away.**

Tickets are sold at varying prices, on the basis of how many trout anglers want to keep for dinner. Lakes are stocked with carp, rudd, roach, bream, tench, pike and perch. The largest carp weigh in at more than 30 pounds. Matches are regularly held, and the site has a growing reputation for the high quantities of fish caught in a day, with 100-pound-plus bags of silverfish taken. Swimming and boating are not allowed.

Camp close to the three lakes that make up the fishery, which is licensed for 10 pitches. Loos, showers and a bar make camping here comfortable. The family-run centre has access to Kentish trails and pubs. Bethersden village has two pubs – The Bull and The George, and a beautiful 15th-century church. The coastal resorts of Littlestone-on-Sea, Rye and Camber Sands are about 30 minutes by car. Folkestone is 23 miles away via the M20. The nearby Channel Tunnel provides a 35-minute crossing to Calais.

## site info

**OPEN** All year

**DIRECTIONS** Turn off the M20 at Ashford/Junction 9 for the A28. Pass through Bull Green after about 6 miles. One mile after Bull Green, turn left into Standard Lane – the fishery is on the right after a sharp bend.

**YEP** Dogs, toilets, tents, caravans, motorhomes, electric, bar

**NO** Shop, restaurant, play area, equipment hire, showers

**ACTIVITIES** Fish

**RATING** Facilities ★★★★★ Location ★★★★★ Water activities ★★★★★

01233 820078

www.chequertreefishery.com

BEST IN Kent

# Gosfield Lake Resort

Halstead, Essex CO9 1UE

I used to come here for family picnics as a kid and in more than 40 years, the old lake hasn't changed much. Fishing and water skiing are the main reasons people come now. Both match anglers and beginners can enjoy the fishing. Carp weigh in at more than 35 pounds, although I've never caught much. Day, night, 24-hour and season tickets are sold. This is a nationally recognised venue for water skiers, who visit from all over the UK. Champion coaches are available for lessons, and tournament spec boats are kept on site. Triathletes also use the park for swim training and open-water swims are held. The 36-acre body of water is no more than two metres deep and it's relatively safe for novices. Swim times are set aside each week and are published at reception and online.

Campers can pitch up at the far end of the lake. The tent field is a bit small and there's no electricity, but the views across the water are beautiful. The touring area has 25 electric hook-ups in the church field next door, and no lake views. Facilities include a toilet, shower block, laundry room, washing machine, tumble dryer, hot washing-up area and chemical toilet area. They are all good, but a bit of a walk. This is the only campsite I've ever visited with an on-site Indian restaurant. A separate takeaway hot food stall serves good food at great value, too. A wooden viewing area provides a nice place to relax with a drink over the lake. The Essex Way passes nearby as it winds on its 81 miles from Epping to the Stour Estuary.

## site info

**OPEN** April to October

**DIRECTIONS** Take the A1017, off the A131 north of Braintree and south-west of Halstead. Enter Church Road in the village of Gosfield and the site is on the right.

**YEP** Dogs, showers, toilets, tents, caravans, motorhomes, electric, restaurant, shop, equipment hire

**NO** Play area

**ACTIVITIES** Fish, swim, water ski

**RATING** Facilities ★★★★★ Location ★★★★★ Water activities ★★★★★

01787 475043

www.gosfieldlake.co.uk

# Coleman's Cottage Fishery 11
Little Braxted Lane, Witham, Essex CM8 3EX

I'm not sure if this is a place for anglers who want to camp, or for campers who want to fish. I do know it's compulsory for anyone pitching up to buy a day ticket as well as the fee for camping. That's fine by me, because my daughter loves to fish here. Just off the A12, the site is in open countryside at Little Braxted, near Witham, on the banks of the River Blackwater. Maldon and Mersea Island are within a 30-minutes drive, as is Colchester.

Four lakes are well stocked with large carp, goldfish, roach, rudd and bream. Each lake can be used with a day ticket, except when matches are on. A tackle shop sells rods, poles, bait and beer. The owner and his staff offer advice, making this a great place for kids or beginners. Pike fishing is available in the River Blackwater, although this section can be difficult to fish.

Both camping areas provide for tents in the top section and five tourers with hook-up close to the toilet block. Facilities are excellent; the only downside is that there are no showers. The licensed restaurant and the toilets are very clean. Nearby Braxted Hall is a working farm where it's possible to buy beef reared locally.

# Seaview Holiday Park  12
## Seaview Avenue, West Mersea, Colchester, Essex CO5 8DA

**Sea, sand and pastel beach huts. When the sun shines (and it often does), Mersea is as good as it gets.**

The island is the most easterly inhabited island in the UK. Access is via an infamous causeway known as the Strood, which can flood for two hours on a spring tide. Locals carry a tide timetable to avoid getting stranded. The salt marshes at Fingringhoe and Wivenhoe, on the River Colne, are a must-see.

Seaview Holiday Park is 30 acres of partly wooded ground sloping to a large private beach. The North Sea waters around the town of West Mersea are as clear as any Scottish loch and as warm as the Med. Swimming, surfing, sailing, kayaking and fishing are popular here, thanks to the site's beach access, a free boat launch and a 100-metre stone and shingle spit. Four-wheel-drive vehicles are taken onto the spit at low tide, but those venturing too far out do get stuck in the mud. Fish for eels, bass or flatties. Long-casting is best either side of high tide with lugworm or ragworm. Trailing a hand line from a kayak or canoe is another option. Deeper water around East Mersea is even better. West Mersea is a great sailing location and there are no problems launching from the beach.

Pitches are on hard-standing or grass, with electric hook-up. Grass pitches tend to be slightly larger. Showers are situated in the static caravan area, so are a bit of a walk from the tourers – they are generally very clean. A private clubhouse and bar opens at weekends and during busy periods in the high season. A café and shop near the site entrance are open most of the time. Dogs are allowed on the beach all year.

## site info

**OPEN** April to October

**DIRECTIONS** Access Mersea Island via the B1025 south of Colchester. Take the left fork after crossing onto Mersea and then turn right on Dawes Lane. At the crossroads, carry on down Cross Lane to the beach and campsite.

**YEP** Dogs, showers, toilets, caravans, motorhomes, electric, shop, bar, restaurant, play area

**NO** Tents

**ACTIVITIES** Canoe, kayak, fish, swim, sailing dinghy

**RATING** Facilities ★★★★★ Location ★★★★★ Water activities ★★★★★

01206 382534

www.holidayseaview.co.uk

BEST IN
Essex

# Waldegraves Holiday Park 13

## Mersea Island, Colchester, Essex CO5 8SE

**Mersea Island is the home of Essex sailing, and Waldegraves is the place to try it out for yourself. The park is off the county's north coast, on the western side of the island, overlooking the Blackwater Estuary. Colchester, Britain's oldest recorded town, is 20 minutes away.**

This stretch of coast offers some of the best sailing and kayaking in the region. Waldegraves's slipway can launch sailing dinghies, speedboats, windsurfers and jet skis. Access to the North Sea and the Dengie Peninsula is on the south side of river. Either way along the coast is a mass of creeks and inlets to be explored. Water is only deep enough for larger vessels two hours either side of high tide. Kayaks and canoes are good to go any time. Swimming from the private beach is safe, with buoys guiding speedboats away. Sea-fishing from the beach is OK. Tackle and bait available from the Wheatgrain shop, at Waldegraves. A boating lake for families who want to bring inflatables or model boats is on-site, as well as four more lakes stocked with carp, bream, tench, roach, rudd, perch and gudgeon.

Several serviced pitches surround the water. A heated, open-air pool is one of the highlights for kids, and there's no charge. A sun deck, lawn and garden area for loungers was recently upgraded. Food is available from the restaurant and snack bar next to the pool. Several outdoor sports pitches and play areas with cargo netting, slides and bridges are good for kids. Dogs can be walked on the beach or in woodland. Abberton Reservoir, Fingeringhoe, Wivenhoe, Wick Nature Reserve and East Mersea Country Park are all within a short drive away. Stour Estuary around Manningtree and Mistley is outstanding and should not be missed.

## site info

**OPEN** March to November

**DIRECTIONS** Exit the A12 at Junction 26. From the first roundabout, follow signs to Mersea (B1025). Cross the Strood channel onto Mersea Island and follow the left turning towards East Mersea. Take the second turning on the right into Chapman's Lane and follow the tourist signs to Waldegraves.

**YEP** Dogs, showers, toilets, tents, caravans, motorhomes, café, restaurant, shop, play area, electric

**NO** Equipment hire

**ACTIVITIES** Canoe, kayak, fish, swim, sailing dinghy

**RATING** Facilities ★★★★★ Location ★★★★★ Water activities ★★★★★

01206 383 898

www.waldegraves.co.uk

# north-west england

**Nowhere has such charming rain. Velvet meadows swell with pride when the heavens open over the north west. Leafy canopies echo with the pitter-patter of tiny, muffled drums, as lakes and rivers prepare for torrents of frothing, silver water that beat about rocky foothills.**

Welcome to the cultural heartbeat of England. Debate surrounds whether Liverpool or Manchester holds claim to the title of sporting/artistic capital. For me, the rural beauty of Lancashire and Cumbria tower above the two great cities as citadels of creative fervour and genuine physical endeavour. For centuries, the north west has motivated writers, artists and musicians.

But boy, can it rain. Seathwaite – just south of Keswick, in Cumbria – sees more than 355 centimetres each year (St Osyth, in Essex, gets 50 centimetres). The driest season is spring, when the Atlantic depressions are at their weakest. When the clouds do part and inland Cumbria basks in sunshine, it's time to wonder what all the fuss is about.

The Lake District is the ultimate playground for water lovers who want to sail, fish, swim or canoe. Derwentwater is one of my favourite lakes. Its stillness is framed by the epic glory of rocky peaks that rise from the water towards the ever-changing skyline. Coniston Water has a quality all of its own, inevitably tied up with Donald Campbell and his fateful last record attempt aboard *Bluebird*. Windermere tops them all – one mile wide, ten miles long and 220ft deep – just an incredible place to explore by paddle or sail; full of character, water traffic and steamers, and more shoreline than any other lake in England.

Lancashire's inland regions are less well known. Bowland Fells is a protected area, spanning more than 500 square miles that form part of the Pennines. Lancashire's waterways remain at the heart of the county's contemporary world. They include the Lune Aqueduct and the four-mile Millennium Ribble Link, which was opened in 2002 to take boats with a beam more than 10 feet long. Its nine locks connect a network of passages including 41 miles of cruising along the Lancaster Canal. The Link runs around the outskirts of Preston and flows into the River Ribble, which passes into the Irish Sea via Lancaster. In the other direction, the Ribble connects with the Leeds and Liverpool Canal, for passage from coast to coast to the Humber. The innovative Bridgewater Canal allows ships to cruise through 'Big Ditch'.

There's not a fantastic choice of waterside campsites along the Lancashire and Cumbrian coasts but the opportunities along the great lakes and canals more than make up for this. Sailing or paddling is relatively safe, fly-fish for brown trout or spin for pike – and it all costs almost naught. A torrent of charm.

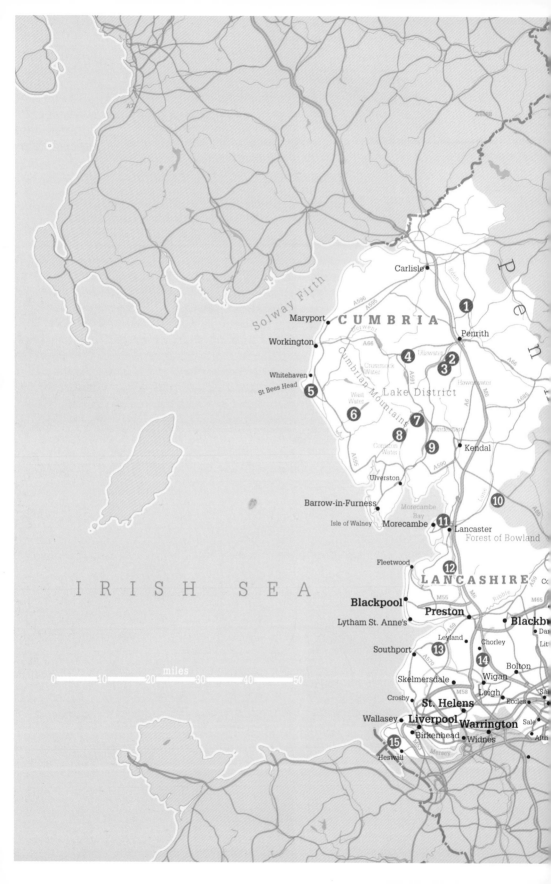

# Lazonby Campsite ①
## Penrith, Cumbria CA10 1BL

**A bottle of claret goes down just fine once the sun has vanished over the aptly named River Eden. If you are lucky enough to catch a trout while fly-fishing, the pub next door is a welcome place to tell all.**

This tiny campsite looks like a crude addition to the kids' playground next door. In fact, it's an addition to a wonderful outdoor swimming pool, hidden behind a red brick wall. The site opened in 1964 and remains one of the UK's last heated, outdoor swims. The camp is run by a charity: the Lazonby Pool Committee. Income from pitches helps towards the upkeep and volunteers help maintain the centre. Community spirit aside, the magic about this stretch of river is the fly-fishing. Buy a pair of discount waders and leggings at the excellent angling store in Penrith, and set off with a rod at dusk. Campers are permitted to fish from next to a public footpath that runs for several hundred yards along the riverbank. Trout feed on the mayflies during late summer. When cattle come to drink at the water's edge it's like a canvas scene by Turner or Constable. Launching a canoe can be a bit tricky, but is by no means impossible. Bathers should take care as the river can be fast-flowing and is unsafe for weaker swimmers.

Farmland partly surrounds the ten pitches in the camp area that's no larger than 15 metres square. Electric hook-up is supplied to eight of the pitches and the night fee includes access to the swimming pool showers/toilets. The pool is open April to September, and the surrounding countryside is good for walking and cycling all year. Kids can spend a lot of time in the community park. Penrith, the Eden Valley, the Pennines, and the Lake District are all nearby. It's also useful for overnight stops to and from Scotland.

## site info

**OPEN** April to September

**DIRECTIONS** From Penrith follow the A6 north to Plumpton. Turn right onto the B6413 all the way into Lazonby. The Swimming Pool and campsite are at the bottom of the village, beside the river.

**YEP** Dogs, showers, toilets, tents, caravans, motorhomes, swimming pool, electric, play area

**NO** Shop, bar, restaurant, equipment hire

**ACTIVITIES** Canoe, kayak, fish, swim

**RATING** Facilities ★★★★★ Location ★★★★★ Water activities ★★★★★

01768 898901

www.lazonbypool.co.uk/campsite.htm

# Waterside House Campsite ❷
## Pooley Bridge, Cumbria CA10 2NA

**Wild and free. There's no charge to fish, swim, sail, or canoe on Ullswater. Nine miles long and almost one mile wide, this is the second largest lake in England. Waterside is a working farm, at the foot of Barton Fell, and has been in the same family for five generations.**

People come here to launch their own craft from the on-site ramp. There are only charges for boats on trailers kept on-site. Canadian canoes, rowing boats and mountain bikes can be hired from reception. A leaflet about canoeing on Ullswater has been produced by Eden Rivers Trust, in partnership with Canoe England. The views are incredible and there are 22 miles of shoreline and beach around the lake to explore. Angling from the beach can be productive during the summer months. Brown trout are regularly caught between March and September, while perch are common from June until March.

Pitches and facilities are superb, but things can get busy during the school holidays, so perhaps consider visiting during spring or autumn. Lakeside pitches are uneven, so bring the chocks. Showers and toilets are kept clean and there's a fully equipped laundry room, although it's a bit of a trek from the furthest pitches. Volleyball and table tennis are free and there's access to a freezer for ice packs. For kids, there's loads to do here. Aside from the fantastic adventure playground right on the water's edge, youngsters can see lambs being born in the spring, and sheep being dipped and sheared. Working sheepdogs are friendly, and are great to watch in action herding the animals. The farmhouse dates back to the 17th century and its land spans almost 300 acres. Penrith is six miles away.

## site info

**OPEN** March to October

**DIRECTIONS** Leave M6 at Junction 40 and follow the A66 for Keswick. Turn left onto the A592 for Ullswater. Turn left at the lake; continue straight on into Pooley Bridge. Out of the village turn right to Howtown. After 1 mile, Waterside House is the second campsite on the right.

**YEP** Dogs, showers, toilets, tents, motorhomes, electric, play area, equipment hire, shop

**NO** Caravans, bar, restaurant

**ACTIVITIES** Canoe, kayak, fish, swim, snorkel, sailing dinghy

**RATING** Facilities ★★★★ Location ★★★★★ Water activities ★★★★★

01768 486332

www.watersidefarm-campsite.co.uk

BEST IN Cumbria

# Parkfoot ③
## Pooley Bridge, Cumbria CA10 2NA

**The best pitches at Parkfoot are next to a creek just a few metres from Ullswater. Campers can launch their own boats and canoes from the private beach. Boats are available for hire next door at Waterside House Campsite (see page 183). Care needs to be taken when swimming or diving. Although the water around the lake edge can warm up when there's sun, deeper watery shelves a few metres out can be very cold, with some parts reaching 60 metres.**

Pitches are available on gravel or hard-standing. Of the three main camping areas, lakeside is best. Noise can be an issue during peak season, although the site owners now impose a 'noise deposit' on potential rowdy campers. Single sex and non-family groups are not usually allowed. Facilities on the main site, across the road, include a licensed bar and restaurant, takeaway meals, beer garden, TV, two pool tables and table tennis. Discos and live music play during the summer. Ullswater Outdoor Festival is held throughout September. Four 'steamers' ferry passengers around the Z-shaped water, which is banked by some of England's highest mountain ranges. The Lord Birkett Memorial Trophy attracts several hundred sailing boats competing across the entire length of the lake in July. Pony trekking from the park and walks on the fells are excellent.

## site info

**OPEN** March to October

**DIRECTIONS** Leave M6 at Junction 40 and follow the A66 for Keswick. Turn left onto the A592 and left again at the lake; continue straight on into Pooley Bridge. Out of the village turn right to Howtown. After 1 mile Parkfoot is the first campsite.

**YEP** Dogs, showers, toilets, tents, caravans, motorhomes, electric, shop, bar, restaurant, play area, equipment hire (bikes only)

**NO** -

**ACTIVITIES** Canoe, kayak, fish, swim, snorkel

**RATING** Facilities ★★★★★ Location ★★★★★ Water activities ★★★★★

01768 486309

www.parkfootullswater.co.uk

# Keswick Camping & Caravanning Site

Crow Park Road, Cumbria CA12 4RR

**Almost the best site in Cumbria. Derwentwater lies against a backdrop of skies and peaks that change colour by the hour. The lake is fed and drained by the River Derwent.**

People arrive to fish, canoe, sail, cycle and walk. Angling can be more productive here than in some of the other lakes. Perhaps that's because, with an average depth of just under 6 metres, it's shallower than most. Fly-fishing from a boat is especially good when the mayflies hatch at the beginning of June. Large perch and roach can be caught, too. Pike fishing is most common from the shore, using lures or flies. Some weighing in at 20 pounds are taken in the shallow bays, but once the weather cools in winter the fish move further out and are best hooked with dead bait. Derwentwater is believed to be the last remaining native habitat of Britain's rarest fish, the vendace. Keswick Angling Association controls the fishing and provides permits. Canoes and kayaks are perfect for exploring hidden coves and the islands. It's possible to launch small dinghies from the site.

As with most campsites in the Lake District, the area is prone to flooding, so winter tyres are recommended. Tourers, motorhomes and tents are accepted, with hard and grass pitches and electricity provided. Derwentwater marina is about is a 25-minute walk away. Berthing is available here for boats up to 26-foot long, with a draught of up to 2 foot 6 inches (keel raised). Daily boat launches ferry visitors across the lake, stopping at seven jetties. Discounted tickets can be bought from the site reception. The nearby Whinlatter Visitor Centre provides the opportunity to watch the ospreys in flight over Bassenthwaite Lake.

## site info

**OPEN** February to November

**DIRECTIONS** From the A66, turn left at the A591/A66 Keswick roundabout onto the A5271. Turn left at the T-junction, then right at the mini-roundabout. Pass bus station and rugby club and turn right up narrow lane.

**YEP** Dogs, showers, toilets, tents, caravans, motorhomes, electric, play area

**NO** Shop, bar, restaurant, equipment hire

**ACTIVITIES** Canoe, kayak, fish, swim, snorkel, sailing dinghy

**RATING** Facilities ★★★★★ Location ★★★★★ Water activities ★★★★★

01768 772392

www.campingandcaravanning.co.uk/Keswick

# Seacote Holiday Park  ⑤
## The Beach, St Bees, Cumbria CA27 0ET

**The beach and rocks at St Bees Head are iconic, as the start of Wainwright's 'Coast to Coast walk'. St Bees is a village resort on Cumbria's west coast, four miles south of Whitehaven and just 40 miles from the Scottish border. Beneath the cliffs, the lower valley opens out onto a mile of sand and stone beach.**

High ground to the right of the campsite defines the changing terrain; a place to explore rock pools, and a hive of activity at low tide. Kids and adults prod their way across the black, pock-holed, rocky mass, clutching their multi-coloured nets and buckets. Swimming can be perilous because of the tidal currents and drawback. Although this is no site for the surfing purist, it's fun for belly-surfing kids and youngsters who want to take their first step up onto a small board. Sailing can be difficult for novices due to the prevailing southwesterly winds. There's a concrete slipway down to the water when the tide is in. Low tide can go out as far as 400 metres from the shingle. Wet sand is firm enough for launching trolleys and four-wheel drives.

As with most campsites that are next to public beaches, the toilets come password protected. If you forget your password, the loos in the public car park right next door are always open. Washing and laundry facilities are well equipped, with hot showers, basins, hairdryers, baby-changing facilities, automatic washing machines, tumble dryers and ironing facilities. A shop next to the site sells basic groceries.

## site info

**OPEN** All year (Holiday Park); Camping March to October (can be shorter or longer depending on weather)

**DIRECTIONS** From the north, bypass Whitehaven town centre on the A595. Then follow signs towards St Bees. At the T-junction turn left onto the B5345. Follow signs to beach.

**YEP** Dogs, showers, toilets, tents, caravans, motorhomes, electric, shop, bar, restaurant, play area

**NO** Equipment hire

**ACTIVITIES** Canoe, kayak, fish, swim, sailing dinghy, surf

**RATING** Facilities ★★★★★ Location ★★★★★ Water activities ★★★★★

01946 822 777

www.seacote.com

# Old Post Office Campsite 6
## Santon Bridge, Holmrock, Cumbria CA19 1UY

**Locals call this the 'true Lakeland'. Wasdale Valley is home to England's highest mountain, Scafell Pike, the deepest lake, Wastwater, St Olaf, the smallest church, and 'The Biggest Liar in the World', elected annually in a competition at the Bridge Inn. The coast and beaches at Seascale are just six miles away.**

The River Irt runs between the pub and camp, and is most famous for its salmon and large sea trout. August and September usually enjoy a late run of salmon. Limited skills in fly-fishing and plenty of luck are needed. Rods and permits are available from the campsite owners. Lancashire Fly-Fishing Association can be contacted for more information on 01706 227548 or at www.lffa.co.uk. The river feeds into the Irish Sea, five miles away, at Ravenglass, where it meets with River Esk and River Mite to form a single estuary. Kayaks and canoes can sometimes make their way upstream from the coast as far as the village of Holmrook, within three miles of the Old Post Office Campsite.

There are five hard-standing pitches with electric hook-up for tourers. The grass is reasonably level. The showers and toilets were clean when we visited and there is a disabled shower/ toilet. A laundry room, washing-up sinks, washing machine, tumble dryer and free freezer make camping here very easy. The site is a good base for walking groups and mountain climbers looking to scale Scafell Pike and Great Gable. A children's play area is OK for ball games.

## site info

**OPEN** March to September

**DIRECTIONS** Leave the A595 for Santon Bridge at the turning just south of Holmrook, before entering the village. Follow road to the end, passing Irton Hall (on your left) and Wasdale Craft Shop (on your left). At the next junction turn left and the campsite is at the bottom of the hill near to the river.

**YEP** Dogs, showers, toilets, tents, caravans, motorhomes, electric, rod hire

**NO** Shop, bar, restaurant, play area

**ACTIVITIES** Fish, swim

**RATING** Facilities ★★★★★ Location ★★★★★ Water activities ★★★★★

019467 26286

www.theoldpostofficecampsite.co.uk

# Low Wray National Trust Camping ⑦

Windermere, Ambleside, Cumbria LA22 0JA

**A proper campsite from National Trust – tents, ducks, geese and bad weather. Views across to the posh side of Windermere, at Bowness and Ambleside are beautiful, but they can keep it. Everyone mucks in here, and the facilities are quality. Sometimes, just sometimes – in any season – the sun comes out and it's like heaven on earth.**

Low Wray is on the quietest north-western shore of Windermere. Fishing is free with a license. Two launching areas from either end of the campsite cater for all but powered craft. Swimming and snorkelling are good fun, but bring a wetsuit. Numerous walks are available from the campsite, with an easy track along the shore. Trout fishing is available at nearby Esthwaite Water.

Pitches are spacious and spread out. Choices range from camping lakeside to being right next to the toilet and shower-blocks. They had been refurbished when we visited. Caravans are not allowed and there's no electric or grey- and toilet-waste point. Pitches are priced according to the size of the unit (small tent or campervan). Things can get quite expensive in a van during high season, as there are extra charges, such as for arriving with a boat or pitching lakeside. National Trust members get no campsite discounts, which personally, I find annoying. This really needs to change.

Camping is only available until the end of October, but the National Trust sites at Great Langdale and Wasdale are open all year round. Two pubs are within two miles of the site. Important N T properties are close by, including The Beatrix Potter Gallery and the Steam Yacht Gondola on Coniston Water. Grasmere, Rydal Water and Coniston Water are a short drive away.

## site info

**OPEN** April to October

**DIRECTIONS** From Ambleside, turn left off the A593 at Clappersgate onto the B5286. Turn left and follow signs for Wray. The site is about a mile on the left.

**YEP** Dogs, showers, toilets, tents, motorhomes, electric, shop

**NO** Bar, restaurant, play area, equipment hire, caravans

**ACTIVITIES** Canoe, kayak, fish, swim, snorkel, sailing dinghy

**RATING** Facilities ★★★★★ Location ★★★★★ Water activities ★★★★★

01539 463862

www.nationaltrust.org.uk
Search 'Low Wray'

# Coniston Hall Camping Site

Haws Bank, Coniston, Cumbria LA21 8AS

Maybe it's just me, but I think there's both an eerie and uplifting feel to Coniston. Donald Campbell's death in 1967 hangs over the water and Coniston Hall looks out across it. This is a working farm with a difference: barking sheep dogs, nesting peacocks, a beautiful lake and camping in the shadow of the Fells with a sailing club for a neighbour. The National Trust owns the Hall and Coniston's three small islands. Entry to the campsite from the road is via a series of tiny lanes that belie the sense of spaciousness you feel as you finally enter the palatial driveway. The lake catches your eye first, then the green pastures that fall down towards the water, then the private marina of yachts.

Fishing, swimming, snorkelling and boating are available directly from the campsite shore. Large pike and perch are most commonly caught. Twenty-pound pike can be hooked on dead bait during the winter months. Lures and spinners from small boats or kayaks are a good option in the summer. Trout and char fishing have declined in recent years. Boat anglers can launch at Coniston Boating Centre, half a mile from Coniston village. Sailing dinghies, canoes, kayaks and larger motorised craft are available for hire but they are restricted to 10 knots. Coniston Hall charges if you bring your own canoe or boat, which is a shame. Swimming in August is usually possible without a wetsuit, but take one just in case. When the clouds roll in, the temperatures drop and the heavens open up, there's no better place to be than in the water.

Pitches close to the lake are most popular but camping right on the shore isn't allowed, as flooding is common during heavy rainfall.

## site info

**OPEN** March to October

**DIRECTIONS** Head out of Coniston town south on the A593. Turn left after about a mile, towards Coniston Hall.

**YEP** Dogs, showers, toilets, tents, caravans, motorhomes, electric, shop

**NO** Bar, restaurant, play area, equipment hire

**ACTIVITIES** Canoe, kayak, fish, swim, snorkel, sailing dinghy

**RATING** Facilities ★★★★★ Location ★★★★★ Water activities ★★★★★

01539 441223

No website

# Hill of Oaks ⑨
## Tower Wood, Cumbria LA128NR

**There is a calmness about England's largest lake. Hill of Oaks, on the eastern shore of Lake Windermere, provides comfortable shelter under the canopy of Tower Wood for when the winds and rains roll over the water. Campers watch the Windermere steamers pass every hour from the pitches (1–4) that slope to the water's edge.**

The campsite beach is a popular meeting place for the families who arrive at 10 am, in wetsuits and sun cream, rain or shine. Small boats, unpacked from the trailer, can be moored pitch-side, alongside soft drinks, bottles of beer and white wine sunk into the sandy shallows. An offshore storage area caters for yachts and powered craft. Controversy has surrounded a 5.2-knot speed limit the Lake District National Park Authority introduced in 2005. The restriction has caused a fall in boat users to the lake. Those left seem to support the ban, as does the yachting community, which has thrived ever since. Campers pay a small charge to launch from the private jetties and piers onto the 11 miles of water. There's no bar or restaurant, but sailing to Bowness for dinner and drinks is a nice alternative. Fishing is free and fun for both children and pike anglers. The kids have more success with the tiddlers.

Most pitches are occupied by privately owned statics, which means the camp can be quiet on weekdays but busy at weekends. Facilities are good, with two large toilet blocks, showers, a drying room and free hairdryers available for the small community of campers. There are two children's play areas. Full-service pitches come with power and water. The small shop sells almost everything.

## site info

**OPEN** March to November

**DIRECTIONS** Exit the M6 at junction 36, along the A590 for Newby Bridge. The site is on the left off the A592 between Newby Bridge and Bowness.

**YEP** Dogs, showers, toilets, caravans, motorhomes, play area, electric, shop

**NO** Bar, restaurant, equipment hire, tents

**ACTIVITIES** Canoe, kayak, fish, swim, snorkel, sailing dinghy

**RATING** Facilities ★★★★★ Location ★★★★★ Water activities ★★★★★

01539 531578

www.hillofoaks.co.uk

# Riverside Caravan Park, High Bentham

High Bentham, Lancashire LA2 7FJ

**A campsite for small fry: a stocking programme for young trout and inflatables on sale. Riverside Caravan Park straddles the River Wenning, close to the market town of Bentham, on the edge of the Yorkshire Dales, The Lakes and the Forest of Bowland.**

Private fishing rights on the Wenning are held by the campsite for about a mile on either side. Brown trout are stocked in the spring as the owners are involved in a programme of sea trout fry, in conjunction with the Environmental Agency. The run of salmon and sea trout occurs from the end of July to the close of season. A lake opened on the far side of the camp in August 2008, stocked with carp, rudd, roach and perch. Daily, weekly and seasonal fishing permits for the river and lake are available from reception. Kids who want to paddle or float about on inflatables enjoy the shallows. Boats and toys are sold in the shop. The River Wenning is a tributary of the River Lune, and is navigable by canoe or kayak. A series of weirs between Low Bentham and Clapham, either side of the campsite, can provide a little white-water fun for very experienced. Clapham is five miles away and takes about two hours by canoe.

There are more than 60 pitches, including a mixture of hard-standing and grass. Toilets, showers, washbasins, a utility room, two laundry rooms and a chemical toilet points are all nearby. Some of the buildings have under-floor heating. The outdoor adventure playground is popular with kids. Gas is sold on-site. High Bentham village is a five-minute walk away and the city of Lancaster is a 30-minute drive. Bentham Golf Club is owned by the family, so campers get discount access to the 18-hole course and bar.

## site info

**OPEN** March to October (and over New Year)

**DIRECTIONS** Head south out of Little Bentham on Station Road. Take the first right over the river bridge and follow road into the campsite.

**YEP** Dogs, showers, toilets, caravans, motorhomes, electric, shop

**NO** Tents, shop, bar, restaurant, play area, equipment hire

**ACTIVITIES** Canoe, kayak, fish, swim

**RATING** Facilities ★★★★★ Location ★★★★★ Water activities ★★★★★

015242 61272

www.riversidecaravanark.co.uk

# Riverside Caravan Park, Morecambe ⑪
## Morecambe, Lancashire LA3 3ER

**This is no place to travel on a full moon at high tide. Riverside Caravan Park is downstream of Lancaster, on the Lune Estuary. The Golden Ball Pub, right next door to the camp, was once known by locals as 'Snatchems'. Ships' captains would 'snatch' drunken locals on their way from Lancaster for overseas trade routes. Today, high tides are the main challenge for unwary travellers. Bore waves can flood the caravan park entrance for anything up to three hours, but there's plenty to occupy the time.**

Anglers nowadays fish for flounder from the riverbank using frozen mackerel as bait. They have most success just before high tide when the river is at its saltiest. Wild salmon are common in these parts (though they are largely protected), as are sea trout, mullet, plaice and cod. Canoes, kayaks and sailing dinghies need to take care, as the waters can be fast-flowing at times. Glasson Sailing Club, based at Glasson Dock towards the mouth of the river, offers good advice.

Although Riverside Caravan Park makes it into my list of top riverside locations, the owners will only accept caravans and motorhomes on seasonal terms. That means a lot of money up-front, for a pitch from March 1 to October 31. Electric hook-up is charged on a nightly rate, whether you're on-site or not. Hot showers and a toilet block are clean. Morecambe Bay to the east and the River Lune combine to create the peninsula that shapes the landscape. Morecambe is a few minutes' drive and the City of Lancaster is within walking distance along the riverbank. The Lake District and the Yorkshire Dales are less than an hour's drive away.

## site info

**OPEN** March to October

**DIRECTIONS** Take the A589 out of Morecambe. Turn right onto the A683 at the second roundabout, and then turn left at the next into Mellishaw Lane. Right at the next roundabout onto Lancaster Road. Campsite is less than a mile on the right, where the road meets the river.

**YEP** Dogs, showers, toilets, caravans, motorhomes, electric

**NO** Tents, shop, play area, equipment hire, bar, restaurant

**ACTIVITIES** Canoe, kayak, fish, sailing dinghy

**RATING** Facilities ★★★★★ Location ★★★★★ Water activities ★★★★★

01524 844 193

www.riverside-morecambe.co.uk

# Bridgehouse Marina & Caravan Park

Nateby Crossing Lane, Nateby, Lancashire PR3 0JJ

**We discovered Bridgehouse Marina and Caravan Park down a sloping, country lane just outside the market town of Garstang. Thanks to the River Ribble Link, the canal is connected to the main waterways systems of England via the Leeds and Liverpool Canal.**

More than 40 miles of the Lancaster Canal's length are easily navigated. Best of all, the entire stretch is lock free, which makes for fantastic canoeing. For longer journeys, the Ribble Link provides access to tidal river cruising. Canoes are put into the canal a few hundred yards from the campsite, at the bridge. Fishing is on the towpath opposite the camp. Self-drive day-launches are available for hire and seat up to six people, for all-weather open or closed cruising. Water and electric are connected to the majority of jetties for some 160 moorings.

The touring park has 50 hard-standing pitches. There is an area for children to play and ducks keep the younger ones occupied. The toilet block is heated and contains showers, toilets, washing and shaving points, a laundry room, dishwashing area and toilet waste disposal point. The town is a 20-minute walk away and the Lake District and North Yorkshire Moors are within a 40- and 50-minute drive respectively.

**BEST IN Lancashire**

## site info

**OPEN** March to October

**DIRECTIONS** Turn off the A6 west at Garstang, into Longmoor Lane. First right leads to the marina.

**YEP** Dogs, showers, toilets, caravans, motorhomes, electric, play area, equipment hire

**NO** Tents, shop, bar, restaurant

**ACTIVITIES** Canoe, kayak, fish, sailing dinghy

**RATING** Facilities ★★★★★ Location ★★★★★ Water activities ★★★★★

01995 603207

www.bridgehousemarina.co.uk

# Leisure Lakes 13

Tarleton, Lancashire PR4 6JX

**Like a kids' adventure park, this site allows youngsters the freedom to cut loose in a watery outback. If yours aren't used to amusing themselves, there's quite a lot on offer to entertain them.**

Two lakes are set aside for fishing and jet skis. One is stocked with carp, bream, roach, perch, chub, tench and rudd. Matches and night fishing can be arranged with the management. The other is for those who want to bring their own jet ski (insurance is needed). A jet-ski service, repair and sales centre is on-site. Swimming, sailing and canoeing aren't allowed. On the plus side, there's on-site paintballing, laser tagging (similar to paintball, but younger kids can play), a golf academy, driving range, a nine-hole golf course, motorcycle and quad-bike track, pony rides and archery.

Pitches are in an area that is part-wood, part-meadow, part-field and part-scrubland. Some people are put off by the high volume of visitors in summer, so consider going out of season. The toilet/shower block does suffer during the peak times. Water's Edge café provides everything from fry-up breakfasts to evening meals. The adventure playground for kids is good. Cowboy and Western meetings are held in the club house, next to the Western Frontier Pub. Southport is six miles away and Preston is 11.

## site info

**OPEN** All year

**DIRECTIONS** Turn off the A565 north east of Southport, onto the B426 at Mere Brown roundabout. Take the first right at sign for Leisure Lakes and follow the road to the campsite.

**YEP** Dogs, showers, toilets, tents, caravans, motorhomes, bar, restaurant, play area, electric

**NO** Shop, equipment hire

**ACTIVITIES** Fish, jet ski

**RATING** Facilities ★★★★★ Location ★★★★★ Water activities ★★★★★

01772 813446

www.leisurelakes.co.uk

# White Bear Marina 14
## Park Road, Adlington, Chorley, Lancashire PR7 4HZ

**Camping on the longest canal in northern England means access to more than 2,000 miles of inland waterways. White Bear is the largest marina on the Leeds and Liverpool Canal.**

Roach, tench, bream, perch, rudd and eels can be caught. A good selection of ground bait and maggots seems to work fine. I've seen other anglers catch fish with sweetcorn and even bread flakes. Boat traffic is substantial. It's estimated there are more than 1,000 craft on the water at any one time. Because the canal is 127 miles long, that evens out at fewer than ten vessels per mile – some way below the national average. A canoe can navigate the entire length, although you must pass through 91 locks and climb a summit level of 148 metres. The West Pennine Moors and their vast reservoirs – a haven for sailing and watersports – are nearby.

Marinas are not renowned for their beauty, but this is a vibrant, picturesque location with multi-coloured barges and their flowering rooftops. Everything is very clean and secure. Newly refurbished showers and loos were installed in 2011. Security issues in the past have been resolved, thanks to padlocks and gates. Ten fully serviced touring caravan pitches (no tents) make this a good stopover for those heading north to Scotland or south to London and the Channel Tunnel. Facilities for the 100 moorings include a large chandlery shop and a marina café that's open until 4 pm. Bolton is about six miles away and Manchester is 20 minutes by car. The M6 and M61 are a few miles away, too.

## site info

**OPEN** All year

**DIRECTIONS** Exit the A6 at Adlington village on the mini roundabout into Park Road. The marina is 200 metres on the right.

**YEP** Dogs, showers, toilets, caravans, motorhomes, electric, shop, cafe

**NO** Bar, play area, equipment hire, tents

**ACTIVITIES** Canoe, kayak, boats, fish

**RATING** Facilities ★★★★★ Location ★★★★★ Water activities ★★★★★

01257 481054

www.bwml.co.uk/marinas/white_bear_marina

# Wirral Country Park Caravan Club  15
Station Road, Thurstaston, Merseyside CH61 0HN

**Wirral Country Park comes with access to the Dee Estuary, 2,000 acres for walking and cycling, a disused railway line, the Wirral Way (opposite the front gate) and an excellent campsite. It's a good base from which to explore Liverpool, too.**

Seven private sailing clubs offer temporary and family membership to visitors. Dee Estuary is tidal, but there is at least a three-hour window for launch and return. Dee Sailing Club is the closest, right next door on the Wirral peninsula, and it is considered a top catamaran racing club. Several members prefer leisure sailing and offer good advice, as does the West Kirby Sailing Club, a little further up the road. Bass fishing from a canoe or kayak is best, although check the status of a conservation zone around the estuary, as this might restrict angling in the future. The beach is OK, but not among the best in Britain – mainly because of occasional litter. Better beaches, at West Kirby and Hoylake, are within walking distance. All around is good for dog walks. The campsite itself is spotless.

Pitches overlook the Dee Estuary and north Wales. Pitch 15 is one of the best for a great view of the sea. The sunsets here are glorious. Of 93 pitches, 49 are hard-standing. Power-boating, water skiing and golf courses are all available nearby. Take the Park and Ride by train from Hoylake to Liverpool.

BEST IN
Merseyside

## site info

**OPEN** March to November

**DIRECTIONS** Turn off the A540 left at crossroads in Thurstaston, into Station Road. Follow road all the way for about a mile into the camp.

**YEP** Dogs, showers, toilets, caravans, motorhomes, play area, electric, shop

**NO** Tents, bar, restaurant, equipment hire

**ACTIVITIES** Canoe, kayak, fish, swim, surf

**RATING** Facilities ★★★★★ Location ★★★★★ Water activities ★★★★★

01516 485228

www.caravanclub.co.uk
Search 'Wirral Country Park'

# north-east england

**England's greenest region comes with dales, moors, Hadrian's Wall, Lindisfarne and an industrial heritage that once powered an empire. Cumbria's Lake District, to the west, may be more famous, but among the north east's many qualities are quiet roads and peaceful beauty.**

Northumberland National Park is one of England's least-visited treasures. Maybe some still associate the region with an industrial underbelly characterised by textile factories, shipyards and coal. Ten years ago I took my parents on holiday to Tees Barrage, a Caravan Club site next to the largest white-water canoeing and rafting course in England. Our pitch was within walking distance of Stockton-on-Tees and less than three miles from Middlesbrough. The campsite was clean, spacious and right next to the River Tees, but old factory chimneys hung on the horizon like dirty washing on a neighbour's line. My dad asked why we'd chosen such a 'built-up' area but when it was time to go, he said he didn't want to leave. We'd spent our days visiting Whitby, Scarborough, the Dales, Holy Island and Berwick-on-Tweed. By night we walked the rivers and canals from the campsite into Stockton.

There are hundreds more campsites outside the great towns and cities of the north. Rural Northumberland is about as far from urban sprawl as it's possible to get. At the Scottish border, the rivers Wansbeck and Tweed rush out to sea. The cobbled city of Durham is surrounded by rivers that flow through the county's towns and villages.

Britain's longest canal – The Leeds and Liverpool Canal – is one of the quietest in England. Spanning 127 miles from coast to coast (east to west), the canal winds its way out from Leeds to the southern tip of the Dales, across the Pennines, and into the sea at Liverpool. From Leeds, the canal links with the Aire and Calder Navigation, the River Ouse and into the Humber. The Ouse flows north for 60 miles via Naburn Locks and towards the fabulous city of York.

Yorkshire, and particularly York, is home to some of the best waterside campsites in the north. Much of that is thanks to the River Ouse and River Foss that meet here, before forking their way out east and west respectively. The coastline from Berwick to Hull provides some of the best beaches in England to fish and camp. The River Tees holds the national record for chub. Tynemouth regularly hosts surfing championships. Other quality surf spots include Saltburn, in Tees Valley. Northumberland's coast has good surf and beach at Embleton Bay, Bamburgh and Alnmouth.

The Teesside White Water Course, next to the Caravan Club site mentioned above, is a great place to enrol on courses in canoeing and kayaking before setting off for the coast, weirs and rivers. The north east of the 21st century is less industrial powerhouse, more space, solitude and timelessness. The Angel of the North.

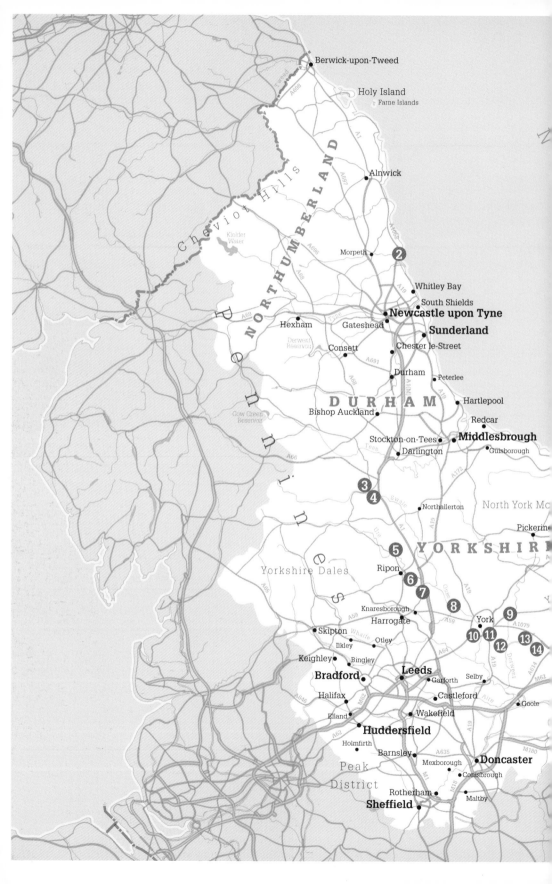

# Stone Creek House Camping & Caravanning Club Site ❶
Sands Road, Thorngumbald, East Yorkshire, HU12 9JX

**Canal-like drains dissect a perfect patchwork of crop-fields on the long and (non) winding road to Stone Creek House. Simon Taylor runs this island site, reminiscent of a Little Venice, at the mouth of the Humber Estuary. He greets guests with a friendly welcome and a passion for sailing, canoeing and fishing.**

The estuary is the coming together of the River Ouse and River Trent. A grassy seawall protects Sunk Island and the camp from high tides. It also provides an elevated platform for views of the landscape and river traffic. Bring your own boat to launch from the Sailing Club next door. The Humber's tidal currents require skippers of some ability. Simon offers advice on navigating the estuary, and allows campers to store their vessels, next to his own, in the front garden. The Keyingham Level Drain, on the other side of the sluice gate, is a more relaxing challenge for kayaks and canoes. The drain was formerly part of Keyingham Creek, and leads to the village, five miles north (seek advice on access). 'It's like being on the Amazon when the sun shines,' says Simon. 'You'll never see a soul.' Large carp swim about the join between the drain, the boat club and estuary. Locals have success with worms and spam. Fish for cod from 60 metres of salt marsh between the campsite sea-wall and estuary proper. Swimming is not recommended, although some do.

Facilities are limited to fresh water, waste disposal and Wi-Fi as there were no showers, toilets or external power in 2012. Electric points are planned to come online for 2013. The roads are quiet, flat and great for cycling to pubs and shops in the surrounding villages. Spurn Head – the unique sand peninsular to the east of Sunk Island – is nearby, attracting birds, marine and coastal wildlife. Hull is 10 miles away.

## site info

**OPEN** All year

**DIRECTIONS** Drive through Hull, over Myton bridge for Withernsea and follow signs for Thorngumbald. Drive onto Thorn Marsh Road and then Cherry Cobb Sands, before arriving on a 2-mile straight road. Camp is on right.

**YEP** Dogs, tents, caravans, motorhomes

**NO** shop, bar, restaurant, play area, equipment hire, showers, toilets, electric (poss 2013)

**ACTIVITIES** Fish, sail, canoe / kayak

**RATING** Facilities ★★★★★ Location ★★★★★ Water activities ★★★★★

01964 630801

www.stonecreekhouse.co.uk

# Sandy Bay Holiday Park  ②

## North Seaton, Ashington, Northumberland NE63 9YD

**Tourers get the best of it on this holiday complex. The campsite overlooks cornfields to the left, and the North Sea to the front. Rocks form the mouth of the Wansbeck River where it meets the coast.**

Surfers and bodyborders enjoy the waves directly from the campsite. An impressively sized boat launch leads down to the beach (I didn't try it out as the waves were too rough when we visited). Kayaking and sailing is possible all along this coast, but local advice should be taken. Fishing on the rocky cliffs below the camp is best after strong northerly winds. Bait up with crab or a mixture of crab and worm, and cast out at least 60 metres.

Pitches have electric hook-up, with access to toilets and showers. Traditional Park Resort facilities include indoor swimming pool, laundry, children's playground, shop and restaurant. Camp facilities include electric shaver points and a covered dishwashing area. Dogs are allowed, although there's a small daily fee. Wansbeck Country and Wildlife Park is a short drive, and has its own council-run riverside campsite. Newbiggin-by-the-Sea is a small fishing port popular for surfing and kitesurfing. The port of Blythe is less than 15 minutes away, south of the River Blythe, where charter boats can be hired for fishing trips. The town's pier is a popular with anglers, especially in the summer.

## site info

**OPEN** March to November

**DIRECTIONS** Take the B1334 south out of Newbiggin-by-the-Sea. The holiday park entrance road is half a mile along the B1334 on the left, just before the roundabout at the A189.

**YEP** Dogs, electric, showers, toilets, caravans, motorhomes, shop, bar, restaurant, play area

**NO** Tents, equipment hire

**ACTIVITIES** Canoe, kayak, fish, swim, sailing dinghy, surf

**RATING** Facilities ★★★★★ Location ★★★★★ Water activities ★★★★★

0843 3092570

www.park-resorts.com/holiday-parks/
north-east/sandy-bay

BEST IN
Northumberland

# Swaleview Caravan Park ❸
Reeth Road, Richmond, North Yorkshire DL10 4SF

**To arrive on the River Swale in the Yorkshire Dales is to be literally surrounded by water – even when it's dry. Not only are pitches riverside, underground springs supply fresh water.**

Fly-fish and canoe on this section of river. Nearby Richmond Falls are worth a visit, and can be reached by road or river. The Swale is occasionally navigable from Grinton to Richmond, but it can be a hazardous journey, with rocks below the water line. Conflicts between anglers and canoeists sometimes arise over differences of opinion regarding access rights. Seek advice, as local agreements, legal interpretation and circumstances can change from year to year. Brown trout and grayling are caught from the campsite. Richmond and District Angling Society controls 14 miles of water between Marske and Great Langton and manages the fishing. Day tickets and week tickets are from Castle Walk Sports, 14 Finkle Street, Richmond.

Husband-and-wife team Andrew and Eileen Carter run the site, which has been handed down from father to son since being bought from a farmer in the 1960s. Woodland surrounds the park. It's quieter during the week, as a large number of the on-site holiday homes are mostly used at the weekends. Facilities include a laundry room, toilets and showers with disabled facilities. Richmond has a Georgian theatre, cobbled market place and Norman castle. Swale Valley Spring Water is so good it's now bottled and sold. The Carters plan to build a restaurant by the river within the next couple of years.

## site info

**OPEN** March to January

**DIRECTIONS** Off the A6108, three miles west of Richmond.

**YEP** Dogs, showers, toilets, caravans, motorhomes, electric, play area, tents

**NO** Shop, bar, restaurant, equipment hire

**ACTIVITIES** Canoe, kayak, fish

**RATING** Facilities ★★★★★ Location ★★★★★ Water activities ★★★★★

01748 823106

www.swaleviewpark.co.uk

# Brompton-on-Swale Caravan & Camping Park
## Richmond, North Yorkshire DL10 7EZ

**Rattle and hum fill the air around camp. The River Swale rushes over fist-sized stones that sound like a million marbles rolling over a waterfall.**

The river is one of the fastest-flowing waters in the UK. Fishing for dace, barble, trout, grayling, and chub is good. Canoes can't usually be launched here as the water is often too shallow. Try the Richmond Road bridge instead and paddle west towards Grinton Bridge. The Swale is a major offshoot of the River Ure, which feeds into the River Ouse and eventually out into the North Sea, via the Humber Estuary. There's a lake park next door, although care is needed when walking around the rocks (I lived to tell the tale – but only just).

There are more than 150 touring pitches, including 27 fully serviced and 40 non-electric bays for caravans and tents. Many of the touring van pitches hug the steeped bank, but there are no river views. An on-site takeaway serves pizzas, burgers and sandwiches. Facilities are excellent, with an off-license, shop, telephone box and post box. Toilets and showers are good and clean. Richmond (which gave its name to Richmond-on-Thames in Surrey) is on the edge of the Yorkshire Dales National Park. The Castle at the town's centre overlooks the river, which is popular with walkers who hike towards the 12th-century ruins of Easby Abbey.

## site info

**OPEN** March to October

**DIRECTIONS** Take the B6271 out of Brompton on Swale. The park is about 1 mile on the left.

**YEP** Dogs, showers, toilets, tents, caravans, motorhomes, play area, electric, shop

**NO** Bar, restaurant, equipment hire

**ACTIVITIES** Canoe, kayak, fish

**RATING** Facilities ★★★★★ Location ★★★★★ Water activities ★★★★★

01748 824629

www.bromptoncaravanpark.co.uk

# Sleningford Watermill ⑤

North Stainley, Ripon, North Yorkshire HG4 3HQ

**A river campsite that has it all: white water, sandy beach, a canoe centre and a reality check. The 14th-century watermill may be defunct, but it bears a timeless message from 1773, inscribed on a stone above the door:**

> *O you that bathe in Lordly blysse, Or toil in fortunes giddy sphere,*
> *Do not too rashly deem amyss, Of him who bides contented here.*

Five miles north of Ripon, the River Ure still offers respite from the 'giddy sphere' of 21st-century living. A Grade 2/3 white water, this section provides a good challenge for paddlers at all levels. River access is free for campers. Fly-fishing is from April 1 to September 30, with trout, salmon and chub all caught here. Day tickets are available from reception for adults and juniors. Calm pools along the riverbank provide an opportunity to bathe but you'll need your wetsuits if the sun goes in.

The 14-acre park is split into three camping sections – the Riverside, the Millhouse Field and the Island. Riverside has electric, hard-standing pitches for caravans and motorhomes overlooking the river. The Millhouse is a quieter area, set back from the river, with mostly seasonal pitches, while the Island tends to be used by families in tents, motorhomes and caravans, with a choice of electrical supply or not. Facilities include two well-equipped clean toilet/shower blocks, laundry room, canoe shop, canoe changing rooms, table-tennis hire, nature trail and shop. Free ice-pack freezing is available. Stands for disposable BBQs are provided at reception for a refundable deposit. The site shop stocks OS maps for the immediate area, as well as for the Yorkshire Dales and North Yorkshire Moors. For walkers, there is a plethora of footpaths. The 50-mile circular Ripon Rowel Walk runs through the camp.

## site info

**OPEN** April to October

**DIRECTIONS** Driving south, take the first left off the A6108 about ½ mile past the river bridge at West Tanfield. The lane leads into the campsite.

**YEP** Dogs, showers, toilets, tents, caravans, motorhomes, play area, equipment hire, electric, shop

**NO** Bar, restaurant

**ACTIVITIES** Canoe, kayak, fish, swim

**RATING** Facilities ★★★★★ Location ★★★★★ Water activities ★★★★★

01765 635201

www.sleningfordwatermill.co.uk

**BEST IN North Yorkshire**

# Lockside Caravan Park  6

Littlethorpe Road, Ripon, North Yorkshire HG4 1TZ

**Blink and you'll miss this one from the road. Once you've backed up, made a U-turn and entered the campsite, Lockside opens up onto a vast meadow sweeping down to the water. The Ripon Canal was created as part of a larger plan to upgrade the River Ure. The canal-side walk on the opposite side from the campsite is beautiful, and carries on for 10 miles along the Ure.**

It's possible to canoe or kayak downstream from Ripon city centre along the canal and down to the weir at Boroughbridge (see page 210). A stop at Newby Hall makes for a nice break. Ripon Marina was restored in 1996 and is worth a visit. Fish include roach, perch, bream, tench, and carp, but they'll test your patience. Angling is only allowed on the towpath side, opposite the campsite field. Ripon Piscatorial Association controls angling, and day tickets are available from Ripon Angling Centre.

Although this is a spacious site, it fills up in August, which can make turning a bit tricky. Beware of driving on the grass during heavy rainfall, as tourers can get stuck. Hard-standing pitches are available. Showers and toilets are OK, but perhaps a little basic. Power is paid for by electric cards. We found that some people liked them and others didn't. Ripon, the North Yorkshire's second city after York, is a five-minute walk away. Ripon racecourse is even closer. This site is a good base for the Yorkshire Dales.

## site info

**OPEN** All year

**DIRECTIONS** Turn off the A61 Ripon Bypass at the double roundabout, south of the Baines Industrial Estate. Drive past the estate on your right and take the first exit on the second of the two roundabouts into Dallamires Lane. The campsite is 120 metres on left.

**YEP** Dogs, showers, toilets, tents, caravans, motorhomes, electric, shop

**NO** Bar, restaurant, play area, equipment hire

**ACTIVITIES** Canoe, kayak, fish

**RATING** Facilities ★★★★★ Location ★★★★★ Water activities ★★★★★

01765 605117

www.campingandcaravanningclub.co.uk
Search for 'Lockside'

# Boroughbridge Camping & Caravanning Club Site
## Bar Lane, Boroughbridge, North Yorkshire YO51 9LS

**I would love Boroughbridge Camping, but I loathe having to pay to put a canoe onto a river. The site makes it into these pages for two reasons: great fishing and no charge for taking a dip (wild swimming). I guess two out of three isn't bad. The town is on the south bank of the River Ure, which flows from high in the Yorkshire Dales.**

Navigation of the Ure is excellent, thanks to the Royal Assent passed in 1767 to build the Ripon Canal. This is a wonderfully still and deep river. Pleasure craft up to 54 feet, with a 14-foot beam, and a draught of more than 4 feet can be accommodated. Roach, perch, dace, pike, chub, trout and grayling are caught camp-side. Closed season is March 15 – June 15. The 10-minute walk to the weir in town offers an alternative challenge: eels as large as five pounds. Locals say you'll need no more than waders on your feet and worms on your hook. If you have no joy, try spam. There are some very big chub in there, too. The Camping and Caravanning Club charges for the launch of canoes from four on-site jetties.

Restrictions are placed on the availability of pitches and the use of awnings at times because of the risk of flooding. There are some all-weather all-service pitches are available. Showers and toilets are well looked after. A grocery shop, a children's play area for under-tens, and a small recreation hall with a pool table and a television are available. The Cathedral City of Ripon is six miles away by road or river. Leeds, York and Harrogate are within 30 minutes. The campsite has easy access to the A1.

## site info

**OPEN** All year

**DIRECTIONS** Leave the A168 on the roundabout directly west of Boroughbridge, onto Bar Lane (1st exit if driving north on the A168). Campsite turning is 500 metres on the right.

**YEP** Dogs, shop, showers, toilets, tents, caravans, motorhomes, play area, electric

**NO** Bar, restaurant, equipment hire

**ACTIVITIES** Canoe, kayak, fish, swim

**RATING** Facilities ★★★★★ Location ★★★★★ Water activities ★★★★★

01423 322683

www.campingandcaravanningclub.co.uk/boroughbridge

# Linton Lock Marina & Campsite 8
## Linton-on-Ouse, York YO30 2AZ

**This 18th-century lock is an adventure playground for adults. Pub restaurant, café, fishing, boat launch, a weir, salmon leap, and passing river traffic. Kids are allowed, but if yours are very young, keep an eye on them.**

The marina looks out onto countryside and the church spire at Newton-on-Ouse. Friesian cows wade down to the river to bathe and drink as part of their midday ritual. Boat and canoe hire are available. Private canoes can be launched from the site for a small fee and larger boats use the slipway, also for a fee. It's fun watching experienced kayakers try to navigate their way down the salmon leap in the summer. Coarse fishing is free to campers, with pike, chub, bream and brown trout all caught. Swimming isn't advised, as this is a busy, working lock.

Both tents and tourers are accepted in the Riverside Field, with hard-standing and grass pitches available. Twelve seasonal pitches generally get booked early in the year. The on-site pub serves traditional food. Toilets and showers were recently refurbished. Showers are coin operated. A chandlery opened onsite in 2012 selling all boat-related accessories. Staff offer good advice on marine issues. New and second-hand boats are also sold. A Park and Ride is available to York. The National Railway Museum and Elvington Air Museum are nearby.

## site info

**OPEN** March to October

**DIRECTIONS** Turn off the A19 about 5 miles north of York. Head west and follow the signs for Newton-on-Ouse then Linton-on-Ouse. Take the left turn ¼ mile before Linton and drive to the river and marina.

**YEP** Dogs, showers, toilets, tents, caravans, motorhomes, bar, restaurant, equipment hire, electric

**NO** Shop, play area

**ACTIVITIES** Canoe, kayak, fish

**RATING** Facilities ★★★★ Location ★★★★★ Water activities ★★★★

01347 844048

www.lintonlockmarina.com

BEST IN York

# Weir Country Park ⑨

## Stamford Bridge, York, East Yorkshire YO41 1AN

**A community of campers on a beautiful site. The River Derwent divides the campsite from the statics. Seasonal campers pitch along the bank, leaving the lake for those who turn up just for a few days or weeks.**

Bait up with maggots or spam on the lake, and pellets on the river. Roach, dace, chub, and perch are all caught with some ease. Pike take spinners during the winter months. Canoes and kayaks are allowed on the Derwent, although there have been disputes between anglers and paddlers outside of the campsite for years. The 17-mile stretch from Stamford Bridge to Malton can be paddled over several days, with some potential for wild camping along the way. A launch fee is payable once, for the duration of your stay. Speedboats are not allowed. Static owners moor their boats on the other side of the river on makeshift jetties.

Twenty-five camping spaces surround the duck pond, with fully serviced pitches for tourers. Showers and toilets are small, but clean. Facilities include a launderette, children's play area and a recreational ground used by dog walkers and kids. Stamford Bridge village is prone to flooding and substantial defences were put in place in 2004. In June 2007, heavy rainfall saw the river break its banks, and the village square filled with water. York is seven miles east.

**BEST IN East Yorkshire**

## site info

**OPEN** March to October

**DIRECTIONS** Drive out of Stamford Bridge over the river on the A166. Take the first right over the bridge and drive into campsite.

**YEP** Dogs, showers, toilets, tents, caravans, motorhomes, play area, electric

**NO** Shop, bar, restaurant, equipment hire

**ACTIVITIES** Canoe, kayak, fish

**RATING** Facilities ★★★★★ Location ★★★★★ Water activities ★★★★★

01759 371377

www.yorkshireholidayparks.co.uk/ parks/weir-country-park.html

# Rowntree Park Caravan Club 🔟

Terry Avenue, York, North Yorkshire YO23 1JQ

**Location, location, location. Rowntree sits right on the River Ouse, next to York. The great walled river metropolis is only a few minutes' walk from the campsite gates. For all its culture and history, the River Ouse dominates the city's character. Sea-going ships once defined York's status as a port of national importance. Naburn Loch means the river is no longer tidal.**

Leisure boats have replaced freight. Although the winds can be unreliable, city sailing is more popular than ever. York RI Sailing Club is based in the village of Bishopthorpe, just to the south of the city centre. A sailing regatta is held annually in August. York Marine, a few minutes drive from the campsite, has a superb launch ramp (see page 212). Canoes and kayaks are common. Care should be taken entering the river if not using an established launch area. York Canoe Club are friendly and meet between May and September from 7 pm to 8.30 pm at their boathouse. There is a charge for non-members. Warm clothing or a wetsuit, a windproof or waterproof jacket, old shoes, and a full change clothes are advised. The boathouse is just off Almery Terrace in the centre of York. Swimming is possible, if a little risky. Several people have died in recent years and there is a local newspaper campaign urging people not to do it. A local byelaw states that 'No person shall … swim in the Navigation so as to cause any nuisance or interference to the safe movement of vessels.' Although most swimmers have no intention of playing chicken with pleasure cruisers, the water quality here may not be quite as good as it is downstream.

The campsite is a classic Caravan Club site – bays are spacious and come with hook-up. All 102 pitches are hard-standing and divided by hedges.

## site info

**OPEN** All year

**DIRECTIONS** Enter York from the south on the A19. Keep left when the A19 forks right and follow signs to City Centre. Keep left at Mecca Bingo and continue over river-bridge. Turn left in 200 metres just before Swan Pub, then turn at caravan sign. Turn right at river.

**YEP** Dogs, showers, toilets, tents, caravans, motorhomes, electric, shop

**NO** Bar, restaurant, play area, equipment hire

**ACTIVITIES** Canoe, kayak, fish, sailing dinghy

**RATING** Facilities ★★★★★ Location ★★★★★ Water activities ★★★★★

01904 658997

www.caravanclub.co.uk
Search 'Rowntree Park'

# Riverside Campsite **11**

York Marine Services, Ferry Lane, Bishopthorpe, York YO23 2SB

There's something quite romantic about sitting in a café on the riverbank of your own campsite, even if the white plastic tables and chairs look like they're from a garden centre. Bishopthorpe is a village two miles south of York. Like York, the village is steeped in history and is mentioned in the Doomsday Book.

The campsite is based beside a working marina, so water activity is constant. Some of the site had a run-down feel about it when we visited, but we felt it added to the overall charm. A large ramp makes launching boats easy and British Waterways Licenses are available. Launch charges vary. Holiday boat hire is available for those that don't bring their own – you can have anything from a motorised launch to an all-day cruiser that carries six people, with a sliding roof, toilet and sink. Fishing is mostly free within the city boundary, but charges apply elsewhere. Salmon and brown trout are common. Swimmers need to take care, as there have been several deaths in recent years in this area. There's a canoe club next door to the campsite.

Tents, caravans and motorhomes are all accepted. Many of the pitches look out across the river. Electrical supply is paid for on a meter and there are chemical toilet disposal facilities. This is clearly a campsite on the up – the loos and showers were brand new in 2011 and construction on a restaurant/bar was due to get underway, although building work had not started when we visited. Wardens are knowledgeable and friendly. It's a quiet base for accessing the surrounding attractions. Bishopthorpe is on the Sustrans Solar System Cycle Track (part of the National Cycle Network and Trans-Pennine Way), which runs from York to Riccall.

## site info

**OPEN** April to October

**DIRECTIONS** Exit the A64 less than a mile west of Bishopthorpe onto the A1036. Drive back under the A64 and take the first slip road off right onto Slimbalk Lane. Drive into Bishopthorpe centre and then turn left into Main Street and turn left. Take third right in Acaster Lane and then first left into Ferry Lane. Marina is down by the river.

**YEP** Dogs, showers, toilets, tents, caravans, motorhomes, electric, shop, bar, restaurant, play area, equipment hire

**NO** -

**ACTIVITIES** Canoe, kayak, fish, sailing dinghy, powered craft, swim

**RATING** Facilities ★★★★★ Location ★★★★★ Water activities ★★★★★

01904 704442

www.yorkmarine.co.uk/camping

# Westerly Lake Fishing & Caravan Park ⑫
## Wheldrake, York YO19 6AH

**This is an adult-only site, where everything is so tranquil that at times I wanted to scream 'fire'. The site brochure states the park is dedicated to fishing, caravanning and camping, which sums it up nicely.**

The 1.5-acre lake was designed by the National Rivers Authority and is fed by local springs. It is stocked with large carp, roach, bream, tench, gudgeon, perch and chub. There is a charge for fishing per day, per rod, from dawn to dusk, and it's excellent value for money. Keepnets and bait boats are not allowed. Anglers enjoy success with all different baits, ranging from maggots and spam to dog biscuits and floating bread.

Pitches in 2012 were also good value and the price included hot showers and awnings. Dogs are 'not really allowed' (unless you've been a regular for more than 20 years) and neither is walking around the lake 'because it disrupts the concentration of the fisherman'. If you need a break from the tranquillity of it all, Wheldrake Village is within walking distance, and York is seven miles away. The Wenlock Arms serves good food and is just a ten-minute walk away in the village. The River Derwent (see page 210) and the Ings Nature Reserve are close by, while the Yorkshire Moors, Dales, Whitby and Scarborough are in easy driving range.

## site info

**OPEN** March to November

**DIRECTIONS** Just west of Wheldrake, eight miles south of York. Camp turning is on the right leaving Wheldrake, right opposite the industrial estate.

**YEP** Electric, showers, toilets, tents, caravans, motorhomes

**NO** Dogs, children, shop, bar, restaurant, play area, equipment hire

**ACTIVITIES** Fish

**RATING** Facilities ★★★★★ Location ★★★★★ Water activities ★★★★★

01904 448500

www.westerlylake.co.uk

# Allerthorpe Lakeland Park 13

Near Pocklington, East Yorkshire YO42 4RL

**New owners took over this 50-acre park in 2011, with plans to improve the camping and watersports available. It is an RYA training centre and it seems set to grow in popularity.**

Power boats, sailboats, windsurfers and kayaks have access to a nine-acre lake. Organised swimming sessions are held in the evenings and early mornings throughout the week. Wetsuits can be hired. Several triathlon events are hosted on the park. A café and wooden balcony onto the lake are a great place to relax while feeding giant Koi carp. Courses are provided in dinghy sailing, windsurfing and power boating, from taster sessions up to RYA level III. Campers can bring their own canoes, dinghies or boats, but must pay a daily launch fee. Fishing is available for both novices and experts at the three-acre lake. Large carp, tench, roach, rudd and chub can be caught from dawn until dusk for a minimal charge.

All pitches are level, have electrical supply and are within a few yards of the main lake. Hot showers are included in the pitch fee. There's also a washing-up area and shop. Allerthorpe's café serves everything from full English breakfasts to cakes, pastries, and afternoon tea. Hot shots can practise their aim at the archery training area. Pocklington is nearby at the foot of the Yorkshire Wolds. The town is home to Burnby Hall Gardens and the national collection of Hardy Water Lilies – the largest wild crop in Europe. Allerthorpe Common Nature Reserve is a lowland heath in the Vale of York.

## site info

**OPEN** All year

**DIRECTIONS** Travel along the A1079 from York until you pass the Barmby Moor turning and an industrial estate. Turn right at the signposts for Allerthorpe. Dive through the village and past a golf course until see park entrance sign on the left.

**YEP** Dogs, showers, toilets, tents, caravans, motorhomes, restaurant, play area, equipment hire, electric, shop

**NO** Bar

**ACTIVITIES** Canoe, kayak, fish, sailing dinghy

**RATING** Facilities ★★★★★ Location ★★★★★ Water activities ★★★★★

01759 301444

www.allerthorpelakelandpark.co.uk

# Lakeside Adults-Only Touring Caravan Park  14
## Bielby, York YO42 4JP

**As a proud dad, I can get defensive when campsite owners extol the virtues of adult-only sites. But this campsite – at the foot of the Yorkshire Wolds, next to the market town of Pocklington – grew on me soon after we arrived. Campers mostly come to fish quietly, surrounded by silence.**

The site has a six-acre lake, designed as a mixed-course fishery. Angling is from 7 am until 9 pm or dusk for a daily fee. Ground bait is by feeder only. Boilies and boilie-substitutes are banned. Pellets or floating bait work for attracting the carp, depending on the weather conditions. Ground bait, soft hook and halibut pellets are sold on-site. The variety and quantity of fish is excellent and the calm atmosphere is wonderful.

Pitches are spread around the water within the 22-acres of landscaped grounds. Toilets, showers and a laundry room are all good and clean. One dog is allowed per unit, but pets are not allowed around the lake. An exercise area is available.

As we left, I made a point of going over to thank the warden. 'It's beautiful here,' I said, with more than a hint of betrayal tugging at my sleeve. 'Thank you,' she answered. 'No kids, you see.' We drove home, feeling like we'd found a little piece of selfish satisfaction in Bielby.

## site info

**OPEN** All year

**DIRECTIONS** Turn left of the A1079 (away from Hayton) into Crudhall Lane. Turn left after two miles, ¼ mile before Bielby.

**YEP** Dogs, showers, toilets, tents, caravans, motorhomes, electric

**NO** Kids, shop, bar, restaurant, play area, equipment hire

**ACTIVITIES** Fish

**RATING** Facilities ★★★★★ Location ★★★★★ Water activities ★★★★★

01759 318100

www.lakesidewebsite.com

# east anglia

**This is Flat Earth Kingdom. From the Middle Navigations to the salt marshes of the Wash, there are almost no hills or high thrills. Just rivers, canals and a collection of peat pits dug in the 12th century for profit by man, flooded by nature soon after, to create the Norfolk and Suffolk Broads.**

Dedham and Flatford have barely changed since John Constable and Thomas Gainsborough captured them on canvas more than 200 years ago and camping around the Suffolk's River Stour is as peaceful now as it would have been then. Thirty miles west from the A12, towards the A1, is High Lodge, where some of the best cycle paths in Britain guide pensive pensioners and wannabe Olympians into the deep and dark Thetford Forest.

The Brecks, to the north, are pine forest and open heathland, but it's Suffolk's coastline and settlements I'm drawn to most. The shingle shores of Southwold, Thorpeness and Aldeburgh are quintessentially English. Lowestoft is the southern gateway to Norfolk. Waveney Valley marks the county border where the Broads National Park infiltrates the land and the area is bursting with wildlife. Entry to the northern waters is via the resort town of Great Yarmouth. The Fens are the region's soft centre – fertile land divided into the open space that defines the Broads and the drained marshes that stretch out towards Lincolnshire and the coast. The Wash is England's largest tidal estuary. Two hundred and sixty miles of coast from the Suffolk/Essex border to Lincolnshire feature some of Britain's finest salt marsh. Surfing in these parts can be good and adventurous boaters should try the intricate Witham Navigable Drains. These waters represent an escape to the very edge of civilisation, cunningly created in one of Europe's most populated regions. I've gone for days without seeing anyone while canoeing these drains. Cambridgeshire is the more refined side of the region. There is punting, picnics and fine student pubs on the River Cam. Fishing on any of these rivers is fabulous.

The spread of waterside pitches across the region slightly favours the north. I've stayed on almost 30 campsites in Lincolnshire alone. Ironically, the Broads – with their 60 man-made lakes, six rivers and 125 miles of fabulous cruising – are not blessed with choice when it comes to waterside pitches. Wild camping can be a good option, especially by canoe. The few campsites there are have good access for sailboats, cruisers and canoes. My favourites range from the larger Waveney River Centre, at Burgh St Peter, to the low-cost certificated locations at either Chedgrave or Beccles where I can pitch with electric for a very reasonable fee. On the coast, the two campsites I've listed at Skegness take some beating for young families. Considering water plays such an important part of the Fens and Broads landscapes, the area is one the driest in the UK, with lots of sunshine around the coast during the high season. Maximum temperature ranges from 20–28 °C in the summer, to a comfortable 5–10 °C in the winter.

What East Anglia lacks in the skyline department, it makes up for with easy cycling, lock-free boating, river snorkelling and those flooded Medieval pits – the Broads.

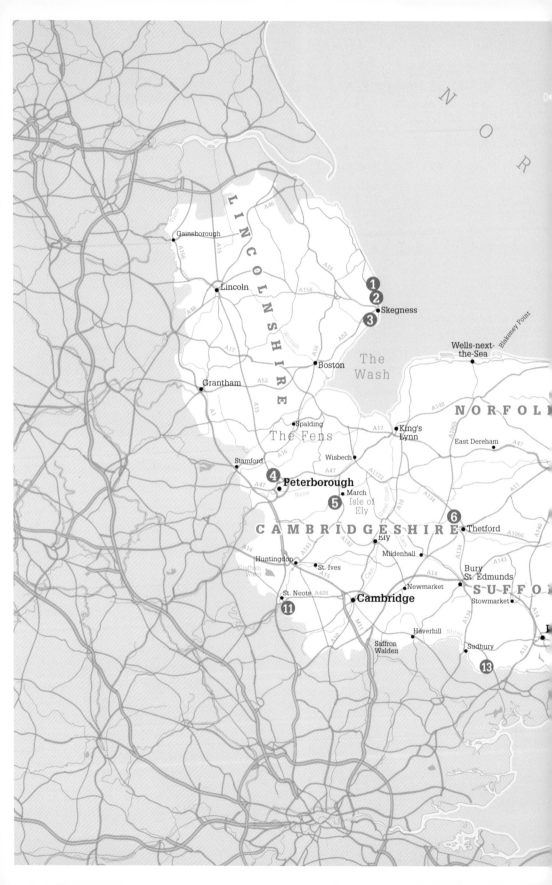

miles
20 30 40 50

S
E
A

roads

A47 • Great Yarmouth

**10** • Lowestoft
**9**

A12

**12**

Orford Ness

stowe

N

# Skegness Water Leisure Park ①

## Walls Lane, Ingoldmells, Skegness, Lincolnshire PE25 1JF

**This is the story of two lakes. One full of fish, the other decorated by winches, steel wires and pulleys. The combination of fishery and cable-tow water-ski centre make this an interesting holiday experience. Skegness Water Leisure Park is north of the town centre, in an area with the largest density of holiday parks in the UK. If it sounds like your idea of hell, turn the page. The park and the surrounding areas are, in truth, a paradise for kids.**

The first lake is well stocked with carp, roach and bream. Pellets are popular among the anglers, with fish over 14 pounds regularly caught. The larger lake is one of only four in the UK fitted with cable-tow water skiing. Lessons, equipment and wetsuit hire are available to skiers at all levels, including absolute beginners. Boats and canoes aren't allowed on either lake.

A large number of statics fill the park, but most of the touring and tent areas are in the best positions, right on the water's edge. Management has an unusual policy of allocating hook-ups to families only, and specifically not to 'young couples'. The brochure claims this is because the camp is primarily a 'family site'. Despite the large numbers of campers, the toilets and showers were excellent when we visited. There's no swimming pool, but just about everything else you'd expect from a large holiday camp is here: an enclosed kids' play area, restaurant, pub, shop and live entertainment. Fantasy Island, with its white-knuckle rides, dominates the skyline, just a mile away. Sandy beaches are nearer still, and for holiday park purists, Butlins is within 400 yards.

## site info

**OPEN** March to October

**DIRECTIONS** Turn off the A52, onto Walls Lane, three miles north of Skegness. The site is opposite Butlin's Funcoast World.

**YEP** Dogs, showers, toilets, tents, caravans, motorhomes, electric, shop, bar, restaurant, play area, ski hire

**NO** Boats, canoes or swimming

**ACTIVITIES** Fish, water ski

**RATING** Facilities ★★★★★ Location ★★★★★ Water activities ★★★★★

01754 899400

www.skegnesswaterleisurepark.co.uk

BEST IN Lincolnshire

# Skegness Sands Touring Site Caravan Club

## Winthorpe Avenue, Skegness, Lincolnshire PE25 1QZ

**Surfing and sea air is a fine tonic. More than 80 years ago, Derbyshire miners were sent here to help heal their lungs. The convalescence home where they recuperated is still standing, between the touring site, amusement arcades and takeaways. Butlins opened its first holiday park here in 1936.**

The beach and surf are the main attractions. Skegness is one of two main surfing areas in Lincolnshire – the other is Sandilands at Sutton-on-Sea. Waves provide good water all year, although autumn and winter are best. Lincolnshire Surf Club, established in 2006, offers advice to locals and visitors on where and when to go. Flatfish, codling and eels are caught from the beach. The three-hook flapper with mackerel strips, peelers crabs and lugworms work well around high tide. Kayak fishing is excellent.

Of the two camping areas, the best is higher up, overlooking the beach. The lower field becomes more popular when the winds whip up along the coast. Hard-standing and grass pitches come with electrical supply and there are a number of super pitches, offering fresh water and drainage. The touring areas are affiliated to the Caravan Club and form part of a larger static park. An indoor swimming pool is free to campers and is open from May to September. Other facilities include a hairdressing salon, multiple shower rooms, launderette and children's play area. A two-metre-tall boundary fence surrounds the campsite with a steel gate leading out directly onto the beach. Campers are given a key to the gate, which has to be kept locked. It's possible to walk or cycle north towards Ingoldmells, via Chapel St Leonards, along the sea-front promenade. South leads towards Skegness via a golf course. The Wash is a ten-minute drive away.

## site info

**OPEN** All year

**DIRECTIONS** Take the A52 north of Skegness. Turn right on Winthorpe Avenue, the second turning passed the golf course, and head towards the beach.

**YEP** Dogs, electric, showers, toilets, caravans, motorhomes

**NO** Shop, equipment hire, tents, bar, restaurant

**ACTIVITIES** Canoe, kayak, small boat, fish, swim, surf

**RATING** Facilities ★★★★★ Location ★★★★★ Water activities ★★★★★

01754 761484

www.skegness-sands.com

# Havenhouse Farm ③

Croft Marsh Lane, Croft, Skegness, Lincolnshire PE24 4AR

**There are two choices for anglers: the river, which is renowned for perch and pike, or when they're not biting, Havenhouse's own fishing lake. If you're experiencing a really bad fishing day (you won't) there's always the campsite bar, open until 11 pm most nights.**

Set in a secluded spot in the Lincolnshire countryside, the grounds of this small converted farmhouse are just four miles from Skegness. The River Steeping is navigable for boats. You can canoe or kayak from the campsite and boat hire is available on-site. Wainfleet village – a mile away by road or river – has several pubs and shops. The river is known here as the 'Haven' or safe harbour, and passes to the north of the village. Skegness Yacht Club is two miles downstream in the other direction, next to the sand dunes at Gibraltar Point Nature Reserve. The club offers good advice on exploring the Norfolk coast, and sits at the entrance to the North Sea and north-east edge of the Wash – one of the UK's largest and most unique salt marshes. Fishing in the river is free. The seven-peg lake is full of carp and bream stocked exclusively for campers, with a small charge per day.

Touring pitches line the riverbank on the grass and there are electric hook-ups. The orchard towards the front of the site caters for tents. Showers are free and there's a toilet and chemical waste point. The Havenhouse Farm serves up bed and breakfast, with the restaurant and bar available to campers.

## site info

**OPEN** March to October

**DIRECTIONS** Four miles from Skegness off the A52, on Havenhouse, next to Havenhouse Rail Station.

**YEP** Dogs, showers, toilets, tents, caravans, motorhomes, electric, bar, restaurant, canoe hire

**NO** Shop, play area

**ACTIVITIES** Canoe, kayak, fish

**RATING** Facilities ★★★★★ Location ★★★★★ Water activities ★★★★★

01754 881555

www.havenhousefarm.co.uk

# Ferry Meadows Caravan Club

## Ham Lane, Peterborough, Cambridgeshire PE2 5UU

**Throw away the car keys when you arrive at Ferry Meadows. This huge site has everything – steam trains, boating lakes, river fishing, two golf courses, a watersports centre for canoeing, sailing and windsurfing, and it's within walking distance of Peterborough. As well as lakes, the River Nene loops its way around the park, linking the canal system and the Fenland waterways.**

Ferry Meadows is the focal point of the Nene Valley Country Park, an area that spans 6 miles, west of Peterborough. Just the watersports centre and lake alone cover 75 acres. Novices and experts can enjoy kayaking, sailing, powerboating and windsurfing. RYA courses and equipment hire are available. There's a café and bar on the lake. Fish in the park all year round, although it's best to first contact the head water bailiff for the Peterborough and District Angling Association by calling 01733 380768.

A whopping 265 pitches are spread across both sides of the road leading into the site – 104 of them hard-standing. The west side has most of the hard bays and is probably quieter. Larger families tend to choose the east side. Pitches are not right on the waterside, but there's more than enough water-fun to justify including the site. Facilities include toilets, showers, laundry facilities, vegetable preparation area, waste point, Wi-Fi and dog walks. Basic supplies are sold in reception and a fish-and-chip van visits during the summer. Wardens are diligent, but friendly. Kids can feed the wildfowl. More than 60 miles of off-road cycleway offer a safe way for the entire family to enjoy a day off-site. It's possible to walk or cycle the three miles into Peterborough along the railway line and river path. Peterborough Beer Festival in August is a highlight. A pub is within a 10-minute walk.

## site info

**OPEN** All year

**DIRECTIONS** Take the A605 towards central Peterborough. Leave on the slip-road just passed the A1139 roundabout. The site is signposted down Ham Lane to the left over a level crossing.

**YEP** Dogs, showers, toilets, tents, caravans, motorhomes, electric, shop, bar, restaurant, play area, equipment hire

**NO** -

**ACTIVITIES** Canoe, kayak, fish, sailing dinghy

**RATING** Facilities ★★★★★ Location ★★★★★ Water activities ★★★★★

01733 233526

www.caravanclub.co.uk
Search for 'Ferry Meadows'

# Floods Ferry Marina Park ⑤

Floods Ferry, March, Cambridgeshire PE15 0YP

**Wild camping in the Fens can be an invigorating, but lonely experience. This campsite on a secluded marina offers a chance to savour the best of both worlds. The River Nene forms part of the middle level system of ditches and sluices that drain the low-lying area between Peterborough and Ely. Little seems to have changed in the last 200 years.**

Apart from occasional river craft, there's a real sense that this is the back of beyond. The Nene's clear waters, particularly along the camp, are alive with fish. Scores of roach swim close to the bridge at the entrance to the site. Eel, bream, carp, rudd, tench and pike are commonly caught. Fishing is allowed from dawn until dusk along seven wooden platforms, and there are no restrictions on bait used. The river runs from Northamptonshire through to the Wash and offers superb canoeing, swimming and boating.

Seven acres accommodate 46 marina berths, static caravans, tourers, tents and overnight moorings. Pitches are on grass and are beautifully kept. Each one overlooks the river. Showers and loos are available. The Mere Eel bar is great for relaxing after a busy day of walking or cycling and meals are available there. This is an ideal holiday for those who can't cope with walking and cycling up hills – the Fens barely rise above sea level.

BEST IN
Cambridgeshire

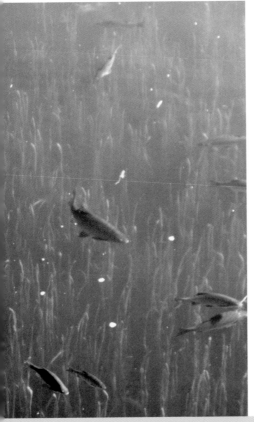

## site info

**OPEN** All year

**DIRECTIONS** Leave the A141 west of March. Travel down Knight's End Road and turn right before the road bridge. If you get the river, you know you've missed the turning.

**YEP** Dogs, showers, toilets, tents, caravans, motorhomes, electric, bar, restaurant

**NO** Children, equipment hire

**ACTIVITIES** Canoe, kayak, fish, swim, snorkel

**RATING** Facilities ★★★★★ Location ★★★★★ Water activities ★★★★★

01354 677302

www.floodsferrymarina.co.uk

# Little Lodge Farm 6

## Santon Downham, Suffolk IP27 0TX

**The alternative Centre Parcs is right inside Thetford Forest. No tennis courts, multi-functional gyms, restaurants or chlorine pools but the fresh fizz of the River Great Ouse and 75,000 acres of protected countryside (Site of Special Scientific Interest) make up for the lack of saunas and spas. Little Lodge Farm is at the end of a mile-long lane in Britain's largest lowland pine forest.**

A ban on powered craft and barges adds to the peaceful charm. This section of the River Little Ouse is navigable and winds its way 17 miles from the River Great Ouse to the Santon Downham bridge. The Environment Agency regularly clears weed from the water to ensure canoes and anglers have access. Camping is a bring-your-own adventure – you need fishing rods, good walking shoes, canoes, kayaks and plenty of energy. Bikes can be hired nearby and a team of ex-army personnel run Ray Mears-style survival courses for adults and children from a small caravan on the site. Bookings should be made before arrival, as they can get busy. Skills taught include fire lighting, trapping, staying warm and fishing. The area is known for zander, which were introduced in the 1950s as a sports fish. The British record for dace was caught in the Little Ouse, at Brandon.

Pitches are in a clearing between pine trees and heathland populated by deer, badgers and raptors. The owners rotate the campsite from field to field along the water's edge. The best pitches are on the riverbank, although the farm has its own Certificated Location for Caravan Club members further up the hill, overlooking the valley. Farm animals graze all around, which adds to the feeling of tameness at the heart of this vast forest, especially at night. Facilities are limited, but unique. You can, for instance, bring your own horse, with access to stabling, grazing and a superb cross-country course. We arrived with a horse in 2010 and paid a very reasonable fee for livery and camping in a motorhome. A toilet and shower is provided. Fresh water and the wastewater dump is in the top field, but there is no rubbish disposal (drive one and a half miles to the civic recycling centre). Two wooden cabins are available for campers who want to upgrade. Segways can be for hired in the forest at GoApe, which is a few minutes away by car.

## site info

**OPEN** April to October

**DIRECTIONS** Leave the 1065 at Brandon and drive along the B1107 towards Thetford. Campsite is signposted on the right, on a mile-long track.

**YEP** Dogs, showers, toilets, tents, caravans, motorhomes

**NO** Waste collection, electric, shop, bar, restaurant, play area

**ACTIVITIES** Canoe, kayak, fish, swim, snorkel, small boat

**RATING** Facilities ★★★★★ Location ★★★★★ Water activities ★★★★★

01842 813438

www.forestlodgeholidays.co.uk

# Gale Cruisers Riverside Caravan Park

## Pits Lane, Chedgrave, Norfolk Broads NR14 6NQ

**To camp here is to have the Norfolk Broads in your back garden. The Broads aren't blessed with too many riverside campsites, so it's worth taking note of this one. It's a good site, with access to hundreds of miles of waterway.**

River boats come and go like rush-hour traffic during the summer months, but it doesn't detract from the calm. If anything, being nosy from the privacy of a waterside pitch is a wonderful way to unwind. Fishing from outside tents and caravans is a favourite pastime. Try not to let the barges or cruisers frustrate you when they scare off the fish. For those that take their angling very seriously, dawn and dusk are the best times to tackle up. Roach, bream and perch will take bread or red maggots. Fishing with worms can hook an eel or two. The on-site slipway is for anyone that wants to put a boat on the river to explore. Most campers choose to bring canoes or kayaks. The marina owner keeps a rowing boat that he lends out free of charge. It's just that sort of a place, but proper paid-for boat hire is available, too.

The camping area is small, at a quarter of an acre, and only accommodates five pitches. This is a Caravan Club CL site, which means it is members-only. Facilities include battery charging, showers and electricity. It's a popular site and some people book a year in advance, particularly during the summer. Coming out-of-season is a very good option. A fine weekend in January can be as much fun as August. As an added winter incentive, hot water is only available out of season. Groups of ramblers meet in pubs at Chedgrave between hikes. The village is just few minutes' walk away.

**BEST IN Norfolk**

## site info

**OPEN** All year

**DIRECTIONS** Leave the A146 at Lodden. Travel north into High Street over the River Chet at Bridge Street before taking the second right and then the third right into Pits Lane. The campsite is at the bottom of the lane.

**YEP** Dogs, showers, toilets, tents, caravans, motorhomes, electric, boat hire

**NO** Shop, bar, restaurant, play area

**ACTIVITIES** Canoe, kayak, fish, sailing dinghy

**RATING** Facilities ★★★★★ Location ★★★★★ Water activities ★★★★★

01508 52027

www.galeriverside.co.uk

# Outney Meadow Caravan Park ⑧
## Bungay, Suffolk NR35 1HG

**The campsite entrance is no picture postcard, but once you get down to the river you'll fall in love with this place. Outney Meadow is on the Norfolk and Suffolk border, between the River Waveney and Bungay village. Campers come to canoe, fish and swim, not admire the front gates.**

Makeshift rope-swings hang over the water from old trees like a scene from Mark Twain's *Adventures of Huckleberry Finn*. The river is clean and shallow, but deep enough to make a mighty splash that frightens the kingfishers. Otters have returned to the area in recent years. Canadian canoes are hired on-site to cruise the Waveney Valley, via the Bungay Loop. Paddling upstream to the road bridge takes about three hours. The river isn't fast-flowing, so it's a relatively easy ride. Downstream (right as you stand on the riverbank) are several weirs and water features that might pose a challenge for inexperienced canoeists. Kayakers can follow the river from its source in Lopham Fen, just west of Diss, to where it joins the sea at Great Yarmouth. For those fishing, rudd, perch and tench are common.

The camp is split by rows of trees and surrounded by conifers, with 45 pitches across the eight acres. One field is for tents, one has marked pitches and the third is a bit of both. Water points, a laundry room, washing-up area, toilets and showers are available. You can walk for miles in the countryside around here and, if you get up early enough, it's possible to cycle to the coast – the site is a Broads Bike Hire Centre. Barbecues are allowed and there are picnic tables around. Bungay is a 10-minute walk away. In town there is a museum, theatre, golf course, swimming pool, sports centre, and buses to the Norfolk coast and Southwold, Lowestoft, Great Yarmouth and Norwich.

## site info

**OPEN** March to October

**DIRECTIONS** Off the A143, just north west of Bungay, opposite the A144.

**YEP** Dogs, showers, toilets, tents, caravans, motorhomes, canoe hire, electric, shop, play area

**NO** Bar, restaurant

**ACTIVITIES** Canoe, kayak, fish, swim, snorkel

**RATING** Facilities ★★★★★ Location ★★★★★ Water activities ★★★★★

01986 892338

www.outneymeadow.co.uk

# Rowan Craft Caravan Club Site ⑨
Geldeston, Beccles, Suffolk NR34 0LY

**An island surrounded by clear water and wildfowl. Rowan Craft is a family-run boat-and-canal centre spread about willow trees and grass but it's more than just a rural, working marina – this is the southern entrance to the Broads.**

Launching a boat is easy. Canoes are available for hire or campers can bring their own. Once you get away, the river is still and peaceful. Beccles is about a three-hour paddle – the low bridge prevents some of the larger vessels and craft from entering the water system, which adds to the charm. Wildfowl and swans roost and feed while anglers do their best to look busy. Bream, eel, perch, pike, rudd and tench are most common.

Pitches are extremely good value, with the price including electric. Although the site feels like an 'undiscovered treasure' on the River Wavenly, it's not always difficult to get booked in. Membership of the Caravan Club is required and there are only five pitches. Showers and toilets are clean, located towards the front of the farm house. The local pubs are excellent. The nearest is the Wherry Inn. The Lock Inn involves a walk down a long track, but is also good, remote, and right next to water. The pub doesn't have mains electricity, so anticipate a wonderful dinner by candlelight. Walks in the area are excellent.

BEST IN
Suffolk

# site info

**OPEN** April to October

**DIRECTIONS** Turn off the A143, at Geldeston, on to Stockton Road. Turn right onto Yarmouth Road and then left onto Geldeston. Campsite is opposite the Wherry Inn.

**YEP** Dogs, showers, toilets, tents, caravans, motorhomes, electric, canoe hire

**NO** Shop, bar, restaurant, play area

**ACTIVITIES** Canoe, kayak, fish, boats

**RATING** Facilities ★★★★★ Location ★★★★★ Water activities ★★★★★

01508 518598

www.rowancraft.com

# Waveney River Centre ⑩
Staithe Road, Burgh St Peter, Norfolk NR34 0BT

**Eddie hangs on the wall in the Waveney Inn. He is a 28-pound pike caught in 1948, and was the inspiration behind the 3.5-metre steel statue next to the Waveney River Centre entrance. Giant fish are rarely caught here now, but the campsite maintains mass appeal among anglers.**

The Waveney is the quietest tidal river through the southern section of the Norfolk Broads and forms the border between Suffolk and Norfolk. Its waters are navigable for 20 miles, out to sea at Lowestoft. The North Sea is reached via Oulton Broad, a relatively easy paddle downstream from the campsite. Powered craft can make the coast in an hour and a half. Upstream is the town of Beccles, with its fabulous lido beside the river. The upper reaches of the Waveney are even quieter, and Geldeston is the limit for larger boats. Water skiing is permitted on some sections of the Waveney, with a permit. Day boats, cruisers, canoes and rowing boats can be hired all year from the centre. Sailing dinghies also have access to a launch ramp. Apart from pike, anglers fish for roach, bream, chub and carp. They have success from the bank or boats. Feeder fishing for the bream in the evening is popular. A good spot is opposite the slipway, at the mouth of the dyke. Fishing from the riverbank is free for campers (closed between 15 March and 15 June). The river is considered to be one of the best in the UK for swimming, although the upper reaches are better. Roger Deakin, author of *Waterlog*, described it as his favourite river.

Seventeen tourers and 35 tents are catered for on-site. Several of the pitches have electricity (bring a very long lead), TV hook-up and Wi-Fi. Toilets, showers, launderette, coin-operated washing machines, tumble dryers and iron are all good. The Waveney Inn, with a children's entertainment room, restaurant and carvery, is right next to the marina. Live bands play throughout the high season. Other facilities include a heated indoor pool (there is a charge), sauna, spa bath, gym and a children's adventure play area, café, large convenience store, and information centre. Don't neglect to walk to the beautiful village of Burgh St Peter. The market town of Beccles is six miles away. Norwich City and the resorts of Great Yarmouth and Lowestoft are a 30-minute drive away.

## site info

**OPEN** All year

**DIRECTIONS** From A146 (Norwich to Beccles) take the A143 (Beccles to Great Yarmouth). Waveney River Centre is marked by Brown signs from Haddiscoe and is approximately 4.5 miles from the A143.

**YEP** Dogs, showers, toilets, tents, caravans, motorhomes, electric, shop, bar, restaurant, play area, equipment hire

**NO** -

**ACTIVITIES** Canoe, kayak, fish, swim, snorkel, sailing dinghy

**RATING** Facilities ★★★★★ Location ★★★★★ Water activities ★★★★★

01502 677343

www.waveneyrivercentre.co.uk

# St Neots Camping & Caravanning Club ⑪

Hardwick Road, Eynesbury, St Neots, Cambridgeshire PE19 2PR

**Big fish and a wide river. The Great Ouse is, at 143 miles long, the fourth-longest river in the UK. I've never seen so many carp outside of a still-water setting. St Neots is a stroll along the riverbank.**

The Camping and Caravanning Club owns the angling rights. Carp regularly come in at 20 pounds. Bait up with bread flakes, luncheon meat, sweetcorn and red maggots from the village. Luncheon meat works best for barbel, while chub prefer bread. The river is navigable by canoe or kayak. Paddling downstream, Huntingdon is about 10 miles away, past the gravel pits and locks. A riverside pub is at Brampton, eight miles away. All canoes, dinghies or small boats must be registered before arrival with the Environment Agency. Take advice first, if swimming.

The camp boundary is defined by the river. Most of the 180 pitches come with power. Toilets and showers are clean and the wardens are very friendly. Don't miss out on the riverside walk to St Neots. Grafham Water is a few minutes' drive away, where courses in sailing, kayaking, windsurfing and powerboating can be taken. If you fancy punting, Cambridge is just 10 miles away.

## site info

**OPEN** April to October

**DIRECTIONS** Leave the B1043 south east of St Neots on Montagu Street from the north or Luke Street from the south. Turn into Hardwick Road and then bear right into the campsite entrance.

**YEP** Dogs, showers, toilets, tents, caravans, motorhomes, play area, electric

**NO** Shop, bar, restaurant, equipment hire

**ACTIVITIES** Canoe, kayak, fish, swim, sailing dinghy

**RATING** Facilities ★★★★★ Location ★★★★★ Water activities ★★★★★

01480 474404

www.campingandcaravanningclub.co.uk/stneots

# Beach View Holiday Park (Formerly Cliff House Park) 🔘12

Sizewell Common Leiston, Suffolk IP16 4TU

**Waves crash against the shore within earshot of campers who sleep under pines. This heritage coast is home to some of Suffolk's most famous landscapes, spread between the seaside towns of Dunwich, Southwold, Thorpeness and Aldeburgh. Energetic hikers rise early to scale the dunes and walk the stony shores.**

The beach is most popular for walking, fishing, swimming and surfing. Whiting are common in the autumn and cod start to arrive during November and December. Anglers bait up with ragworm and lugworm, peeler crab and squid. Crabs can be a problem stealing bait. Summer is best for bass and sole, just before high tide. Canoes and kayaks launch from the beach. For trolling from a kayak, the smallest rubber, fake-fish lures, seem to work best on a calm day – especially when the bass are feeding on the surface of the water. Thorpeness, a mile south, is better for dinghies, as it is built next to a Victorian mere. Boats can be hired there, too.

Tents, touring caravans, static holiday homes and log cabins make up the accommodation. This is a pull-up-and-park family site. The camping field is large, relatively flat and with no specific marked pitches. Hot showers are included in the price. Commercial quality washers and a dryer (for a fee) are available in the laundry room. A fridge and freezer are free for anyone. The site restaurant and bar has views across the beach. Wi-Fi comes with a small charge. The RSPB bird sanctuary at Minsmere is within driving distance.

## site info

**OPEN** March to November

**DIRECTIONS** Leave the A12 at Saxmundham onto the A1121. Take the A1119 to Leiston. Drive through Leiston via King George's Avenue. Turn right at the T-junction before taking the first right and then first left into the campsite.

**YEP** Dogs, showers, toilets, tents, caravans, motorhomes, electric, bar, restaurant, play area

**NO** Equipment hire, shop

**ACTIVITIES** Canoe, kayak, fish, swim, surf

**RATING** Facilities ★★★★★ Location ★★★★★ Water activities ★★★★★

01728 830724

www.beachviewholidaypark.co.uk

# Rushbanks Farm 13

Bures Road, Wissington, Suffolk CO6 4NA

**Rushbanks Farm lies in a small valley beneath a row of cottages, on the Suffolk side of the River Stour between Bures and Nayland. Apart from being a waterhole for wild swimming and canoeing, it's stunningly beautiful. People travel from all over the UK to navigate the 25 miles from Sudbury to the Cattawade Barrier each September. The Stour passes through some of Essex's most famous beauty spots, including Constable Country at Flatford, and Cattawade, near Manningtree and Mistley.**

Rushbanks is the only campsite on this picturesque river valley, which became part of a commercial waterway in 1705 but has long since been cleaned up. Wild swimmers enjoy sharing the water with fish and paddlers. Launching or swimming is easy, as this is one of the widest sections of river, with about a mile and a half of unobstructed access. Several of the locks from Sudbury to the sea have now disappeared, but the annual Sudbury to Sea (S2C) event keeps the river open, thanks to the excellent work of the River Stour Trust. It's possible to paddle 12 miles to the sea or about 15 miles further inland.

A metal gate opens up onto the dirt-track that leads from the road down to the water. Because it's a working farm, dogs have to be kept on leads. Facilities are limited and there's no electric. Although tents are accepted, the farmer, Garth Bates, encourages campers to provide their own sanitation. Mr Bates is a member of the River Stour Trust. He provides fresh water and there's a pit for wastewater. Several good pubs are nearby.

## site info

**OPEN** April to October

**DIRECTIONS** From Colchester take the A134 to Nayland. At Nayland turn left, Sign posted 'Bures'. Follow the road for one and a half miles past a sign for 'Wissington Church'. Follow the campsite sign at the group of cottages on the left.

**YEP** Dogs, tents, caravans, motorhomes

**NO** Shower, electric, shop, bar, restaurant, play area

**ACTIVITIES** Canoe, kayak, fish, swim, small boat

**RATING** Facilities ★★★★★ Location ★★★★★ Water activities ★★★★★

078 6032 5064

www.riverstourboating.org.uk/campsite.htm

# index